CONTENTS

CHAPTER 1

The Invisible Hand

CHAPTER 2

CHAPTER 3

CHAPTER 4

CHAPTER 5

CHAPTER 6

CHAPTER 7

CHAPTER 8

FOREWORD

Sitting in the green room at NBC's *Today Show* in New York City, preparing to do a segment on my new book *Debt Free for Life*, I met Charles Kochman, editorial director of Abrams ComicArts. Charlie asked if I would consider reviewing a new book they had coming out called *Economix* by Michael Goodwin. My first thought was, *A graphic book on the economy—that sounds cool. But seriously?* How in the world can you take a subject as complicated as the history of economics and explain it graphically? "Graphically" is really just another word for "adult comic book," right? For that matter, can you really make learning about the history of the economy easy and entertaining enough that people will want to read it?

As I was thinking about this, I met another *Today Show* guest, Jeff Kinney, author of the *Diary of a Wimpy Kid* series, who was also published by Abrams. Kinney's books had single-handedly gotten my seven-year-old son, Jack, to *love* reading. I took a picture with Jeff, asked for his autograph for my son, and it hit me: *Economix* could be a complete game changer. If you could write a book that explains the history of the economy and make that information approachable, millions could benefit! The more I thought

about this, the more certain I became that *Economix* could help tens of millions—if it was any good. I left the *Today Show* still skeptical but also interested and excited about the potential of how a book like this could serve so many.

A couple of weeks later, Abrams sent *Economix* to my office to review. I had planned to flip through it, then come back to it later. In three hours I had read the entire book cover to cover. All I can say is that I wish I'd had this book twenty-five years ago when I was graduating college. It's simply phenomenal!

Economix does what I have never seen done before: it breaks down the history of global economics in a concise, easy, and entertaining read. Let's face it: even if you *love* economics as I do, and you study this stuff, it can be difficult and often boring. *Economix* isn't boring; it's the exact opposite. It's eye-opening, exciting, and powerfully educational—and, most important, a fantastic, fast, and fun read.

Economix is also a time-saver: you could read ten books on the subject and not glean this much information. Michael Goodwin has done an exhaustive study of economic history and then masterfully summarized and explained it. Add in Dan Burr, who did the most incredible job of illustrating the prose, and you've now got the ultimate fun crash course in the history of the economy. It's almost not fair, when I think how lucky young people are to get this book in their hands. You'll get to benefit from this read without all the pain and suffering that the rest of us went through to learn this stuff. I'm jealous. But I am also truly delighted and honored to share this book and provide the foreword.

I can tell you for a fact that this book will be required reading for my two young boys, Jack and James. I have taken multiple economics courses in college and studied personal finance for over two decades, and I've simply never seen the history of economics explained this well. My sons will have a leg up on their friends by reading and understanding how economic issues affect them and how economic forces have shaped history and will impact their future.

With the recent recession, we've learned that the economy affects us all. What happens in Greece in 2012 affects us on Main Street and Wall Street in the USA—but why? The Federal Reserve says interest rates will stay low until 2014, but what can that do to our deficit, job growth, housing, and on and on? How did the mortgage crisis really happen? Why did Lehman Brothers go bankrupt? Each year, each month, each day, something happens in the economy that impacts us. It is critical that more people understand the basis of how the economy works so that more people can provide intelligent input and actions. There is

simply too much economic rhetoric today that is politically biased and media driven. What's needed is thoughtful discussion about what has worked and what hasn't worked in the past. More people need this information—and now more people can access it.

The economy matters. That idea is not a political slogan but rather a lifeline of financial well-being. I have always said that the first economy you should worry about and focus on is your own economy. But the reality is that you do need to understand how the economy has worked in the past and how it's working now. The more you understand the economy, the better you can manage your own economy—and I believe *Economix* can help you do just that.

I truly loved this book, and I plan to pass it along to everyone who will listen. This book needs to be required reading in high schools and colleges—but the best place to start educating our young people is at home. So buy this book, read it, and share it with your family. Go make your own economy bright and powerful—because it can be—and history proves it.

Live and finish rich,
David Bach

DAVID BACH is the founder of FinishRich.com and the author of nine *New York Times* bestsellers, including *Debt Free for Life*; *The Automatic Millionaire;* and *Start Late, Finish Rich.*

INTRODUCTION

"We're citizens of a democracy," Michael Goodwin's comic persona says in the opening pages of *Economix*. "Most of the issues we vote on come down to economic issues. It's our responsibility to understand what we are voting about." *Economix* will help you understand. It will enable you to grasp the bigger picture and smaller details of economics and economies. It will also make you laugh. It is, after all, a comic book, and a large part of its brilliance is in the way it brings to life, through clever, humorous, and engaging illustrations, a set of quite complicated and difficult ideas and arguments. With *Economix*, Goodwin has done the seemingly impossible—he has made economics comprehensible *and* funny.

But *Economix* is more than just entertaining exposition. It is an exposé as well. Goodwin argues that, at least since the work of David Ricardo, a nineteenth-century economist ("possibly the most important person nobody's ever heard of"), mainstream economics, with its central faith in free markets, has reflected and served the partial interests of wealth and power, while being packaged for the public as universal truth.

That message is crucial for us today. By the late 1970s, most economists and policy makers had committed to the view that markets should be freer and governments smaller. Margaret Thatcher and Ronald Reagan swept to power on that plank, and each notoriously rolled back regulations, slashed and privatized public services, minimized corporate taxes, and bargained away economic sovereignty in the name of "free trade."

Such measures were necessary, the public was told, because, according to prevailing economic wisdom, free markets were the surest path to prosperity. Without interference from governments, in the forms of regulation, taxation, and spending, the argument went (and *still* goes), markets would adjust prices, wages, employment, and production in the most efficient and socially beneficial ways and make life better for everyone.

Yet, as Goodwin shows, the promises of economists were, and continue to be, profoundly belied by the facts. Over the last thirty years, many people became poorer; the middle class collapsed; sovereign debt, including that of the United States, exploded; workers lost benefits and bargaining power, not to mention jobs (now America's leading export); global warming and environmental degradation reached crisis levels; corporations became corrupt, criminal, and dysfunctional

(Remember Enron and the 2008 Wall Street meltdown?); public institutions and infrastructure—arguably democracy itself—deteriorated; and the intangible values of community succumbed to hyper-consumerism.

In short, we are today, once again, suffering the painful effects of economic delusion. That is why *Economix*, a powerful antidote to that delusion, is such a timely and important book. Read *Economix*. Learn from it. Enjoy it. Tell others to read it. And don't be surprised if it turns out to be the first comic book to win its author the Nobel Prize in Economics.

—*Joel Bakan*

JOEL BAKAN is a professor of law at the University of British Columbia and the author of *The Corporation: The Pathological Pursuit of Profit and Power*, which was also made into an award-winning documentary.

PREFACE

I WENT BACK TO THE *ORIGINAL SOURCES*, THE GREAT ECONOMISTS,

ADAM SMITH
THOMAS MALTHUS
DAVID RICARDO
FRIEDRICH ENGELS
ALFRED MARSHALL
JOHN MAYNARD KEYNES
KARL MARX

and started to see a *big picture*.

!

And while the whole picture was complicated, no one part of it was all that hard to understand.

PEOPLE SHOULD *KNOW* THIS!

I could see that all this information made a story. But I couldn't find a book that told the story in an accessible way. So I decided to write one, in the most accessible form I knew: comics.

I BELIEVE THAT WE *CAN* UNDERSTAND THE STORY OF THE ECONOMY, AND IT'S NEVER BEEN MORE IMPORTANT THAT WE DO. WE'VE TRIED LEAVING THE ECONOMY TO OTHERS TO UNDERSTAND; THAT'S WHY WE'RE IN THE MESS WE'RE IN.

We're citizens of a democracy. Most of the issues we vote on come down to *economics*. It's our *responsibility* to understand what we're voting about.

9

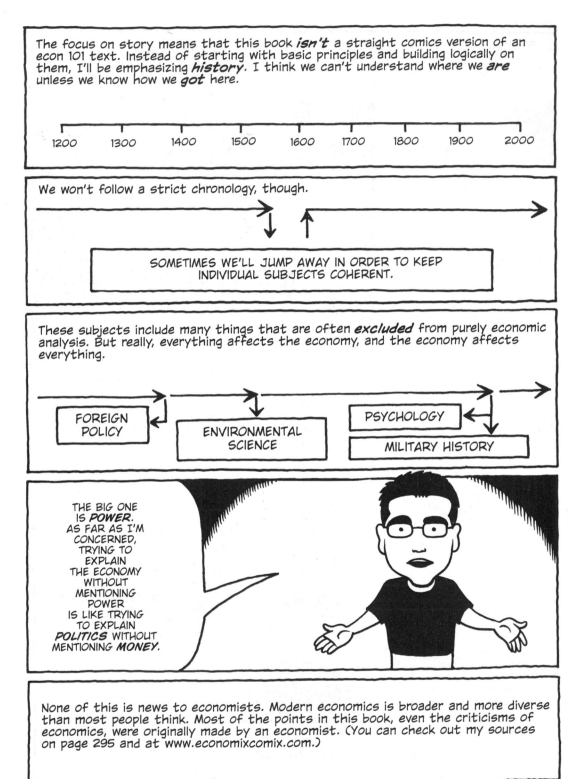

The focus on story means that this book **isn't** a straight comics version of an econ 101 text. Instead of starting with basic principles and building logically on them, I'll be emphasizing **history**. I think we can't understand where we **are** unless we know how we **got** here.

1200   1300   1400   1500   1600   1700   1800   1900   2000

We won't follow a strict chronology, though.

SOMETIMES WE'LL JUMP AWAY IN ORDER TO KEEP INDIVIDUAL SUBJECTS COHERENT.

These subjects include many things that are often **excluded** from purely economic analysis. But really, everything affects the economy, and the economy affects everything.

FOREIGN POLICY

ENVIRONMENTAL SCIENCE

PSYCHOLOGY

MILITARY HISTORY

THE BIG ONE IS **POWER**. AS FAR AS I'M CONCERNED, TRYING TO EXPLAIN THE ECONOMY WITHOUT MENTIONING POWER IS LIKE TRYING TO EXPLAIN **POLITICS** WITHOUT MENTIONING **MONEY**.

None of this is news to economists. Modern economics is broader and more diverse than most people think. Most of the points in this book, even the criticisms of economics, were originally made by an economist. (You can check out my sources on page 295 and at www.economixcomix.com.)

POINT BEING, PEOPLE WHO THINK THAT THE ECONOMY IS A FIXED SET OF LOGICAL RULES THAT ONLY MATH GENIUSES CAN UNDERSTAND ARE A MINORITY. THEY'RE ALSO WRONG.

AFTER ALL, ECONOMICS ISN'T CHEMISTRY—IT DEALS WITH THE INFINITE COMPLEXITY OF *HUMAN BEHAVIOR*, NOT WITH RIGID LAWS.

THAT'S WHY I HAVE *MYSELF* NARRATING. THIS BOOK IS MY TAKE ON THINGS ECONOMIC, FOR BETTER OR WORSE. FOR INSTANCE, WHILE I *TRIED* TO COVER THE WHOLE WORLD, I FOCUSED ON THE ECONOMY OF THE UNITED STATES BECAUSE I'M AN AMERICAN AND THAT'S THE ECONOMY I LIVE IN.

FOR THAT MATTER, *EVERY* BOOK ON THE ECONOMY IS SOMEONE'S PERSONAL TAKE ON THINGS. SO DON'T TREAT THIS BOOK—OR ANY OTHER—AS GOSPEL. IF SOMETHING SEEMS *WRONG*, IT'S NEVER BEEN EASIER TO CHECK FACTS, FIND OTHER OPINIONS, AND THINK THINGS THROUGH YOURSELF.

AFTER ALL, SOME PEOPLE KNOW LOTS ABOUT THE ECONOMY, SOME KNOW A LITTLE, BUT *NOBODY* UNDERSTANDS THE WHOLE THING, AND *ANYONE* CAN UNDERSTAND IT BETTER.

WHICH IS WHY I WROTE THIS BOOK!

Where to begin? Well, everyone says we live in a *capitalist* economy, so let's go back a few centuries and look at *capitalism*.

Every individual is continually exerting himself to find out the most advantageous employment for whatever capital he can command. It is his own advantage, indeed, and not that of the society, which he has in view. But the study of his own advantage naturally, or rather necessarily, leads him to prefer that employment which is most advantageous to the society.

—Adam Smith, *The Wealth of Nations* (1776)

CHAPTER 1

THE
INVISIBLE
HAND

(The Distant Past to 1820)

CAPITAL, CAPITALISTS, AND CAPITALISM

Capital is the means of production. The word often refers to capital goods, which are the things we make, not because we want them for themselves, but because they help us make the things we do want.

FACTORIES
TRADING SHIPS
TOOLS
SEEDS
POTTERY WHEELS
PLOUGHS
ETC.

Capital also refers to the money we spend to buy or rent land, labor, and capital goods in order to start making something. Spending money on capital is called *investment*.

WORKERS' SALARIES

RENT FOR WORKSHOP

EQUIPMENT

The point of investment is to sell your product for **more** than you invested in it and earn a **profit**.

YOU HAVE TO SPEND MONEY TO MAKE MONEY!

Someone who lives by investing money for profit is called a **capitalist**.

Capitalists don't need to invest their own money—they can borrow **someone else's money** . . .

BORROWED

by paying interest.

PAID BACK

So capitalists don't need capital, exactly. What they need is the guts to undertake new projects.

I'M AN *UNDERTAKER!*

HMM. SAY IT IN FRENCH.

I'M AN *ENTREPRENEUR!*

Now: Capitalists have been around for millennia, but the capitalist economy is fairly recent. For most of history, most people lived in farming economies governed by *tradition*.

New projects were often *frowned* on.

NEW THINGUMAWATCHIT! FOR SALE

Also, investing isn't the same thing as saving. To save, you hold on to your money. To invest, you let it go.

Letting go of your savings is risky. In the farming economies of the past, it was often *very risky*, so people often saved their money *without* investing it.

Capital, capitalists, and things that took a lot of capital to make, such as *metal* goods, were often rare. Which is one reason medieval barbers were also *surgeons*.

WAIT—*WHAT* ARE YOUR QUALIFICATIONS?

MY RAZOR'S THE ONLY SHARP BLADE IN TOWN!

THAT'S *IT?*

Nobody likes risk. Over the centuries, capitalists invented ways to make investing *less* risky, like **banking**.

Many people save their money in the bank.

The bank invests it in so many projects that there's almost no chance of them *all* failing.

Bank

mine

By the 17th century, the **Dutch** were making good use of banking, insurance, and other capitalist innovations. They *organized their economy* around trade and manufacturing more than around farming.

NETHERLANDS

GERMANY

BELGIUM

Dutch businesses were so efficient that they **ruled Europe's trade** – even people *at war* with the Dutch still bought goods from them.

THEY HAVE THE BEST DEALS!

This **vexed** some people.

WE BUY SUPPLIES FROM THE DUTCH, WHO USE OUR MONEY TO HIRE AN ARMY TO BEAT US! IT'S NOT FAIR!

Enter **Jean-Baptiste Colbert** (1619-1683), who became finance minister of France in 1665. He thought **money** was **wealth**, end of story.

"EVERYONE . . . AGREES THAT THE MIGHT AND GREATNESS OF A STATE IS MEASURED ENTIRELY BY THE QUANTITY OF SILVER IT POSSESSES."

In this book, direct quotes will be in italics with quotation marks. Otherwise I'm, um, putting words in people's mouths.

Colbert wanted to keep foreign hands off France's money.

ESPECIALLY DUTCH HANDS!

This meant:

SUBSIDIES FOR EXPORTS

TAXES ON IMPORTS (*TARIFFS*)

HOW TO WEAVE

YOUR FABRIC MUST CONTAIN EXACTLY 1,408 THREADS!

REGULATIONS FOR FRENCH BUSINESSES (SO THEIR PRODUCTS WERE GOOD ENOUGH TO COMPETE WITH DUTCH ONES)

DUTCH GO HOME

NO DUTCH

SCHEERJE WEG!

Colbert's *mercantilism*— government controls favoring homegrown merchants—caught on...

and it helped knock the Dutch down a peg. By 1672 the Dutch were so stressed that they flipped out and *ate their prime minister*.

AS THE DUTCH DECLINED AS AN ECONOMIC POWER, BRITAIN AND FRANCE FOUGHT TO TAKE THEIR PLACE.

Wars require financing, and the British government usually managed to raise almost as much money as the French, even though France had *triple* Britain's population. By the 1700s, French thinkers were wondering *why*.

WE SHOULD BE RICHER THAN THOSE BRITISH. WHAT'S GOING ON?

THE PHYSIOCRATS

French thinking on economics changed. Maybe wealth wasn't a stockpile of silver like Colbert thought. Maybe wealth *circulated*, like blood circulates through a body. Laws, regulations, tariffs, subsidies, and so on would get in the way of that natural circulation.

BETTER TO *LEAVE IT ALONE . . .*

Francois Quesnay (1694–1774), physician and Philosopher

Or in French:

LAISSEZ-FAIRE!

Few people had really looked at the circulation of wealth on its own terms before. The Frenchmen who did called their new field of study *political economy*; they called themselves *economists* (also *physiocrats*, from the Greek for "rule by nature"). Physiocrats believed wealth was governed by natural mechanical laws just like the rest of the universe.

But when the physiocrats tried to explain *how* wealth circulated . . .

THE ECONOMIC TABLE OF
DR. FRANCOIS QUESNAY (1759)

600 reproduce net

	HALF GOES HERE	HALF GOES HERE	
300			300
150			150
75			75
37.5			37.5
18.75			18.75

SEE?

THAT'S PRETTY WACKY; HERE IT IS *DECODED* (YOU'LL HAVE TO TAKE MY WORD FOR IT).

FARMERS *MAKE* THE WEALTH.	LANDLORDS *TAKE* IT.	EVERYONE ELSE IS IRRELEVANT.
300		300
150		150
75		75
37.5		37.5
18.75		18.75

Quesnay's table was actually a decent description of the **farming** economy France was growing out of. And much of France hadn't grown out of it yet.

SEE?

But the *real* story was the rising capitalist economy.

SHIPPER
SMITH
INSURANCE
BAKER
BUTCHER
BREWER
BANK

Who would explain capitalism? Let's cross the English Channel and check out a Scottish economist, *Adam Smith* (1723-1790).

ADAM SMITH AND THE FREE MARKET

Smith's revolutionary work:

AN INQUIRY INTO THE NATURE AND CAUSES OF THE WEALTH OF NATIONS (1776)

To Smith, one cause of wealth was **the *division of labor*.** He described a workshop where 10 workers made nothing but pins.

| DRAWS OUT WIRE | STRAIGHTENS WIRE | SHARPENS POINT | PUTS HEAD ON | AND SO ON. |

TOGETHER THEY MADE 48,000 PINS A DAY—FAR MORE THAN TEN PEOPLE COULD MAKE IF EACH WORKED ALONE.

I CAN'T EVEN MAKE *ONE!*

The pin workshop had a clear organization—one person gave the orders.

BUT WHO GAVE THE ORDERS TO ALL THE PEOPLE WHO WORKED ON BIGGER TASKS, LIKE MAKING A LOAF OF BREAD?

BAKERY

BREAD / 3 PENCE

Nobody did. Bakers didn't work because some Bread Planner told them to, or because they were saints who wanted people to be well fed. They worked because it was good for **them**.

"IT IS NOT FROM THE BENEVOLENCE OF THE BUTCHER, THE BREWER, AND THE BAKER, THAT WE EXPECT OUR DINNER, BUT FROM THEIR REGARD TO THEIR OWN INTEREST."

But if the baker cared only about himself, why didn't he do **this**?

BREAD / 10 PENCE

Smith's answer:

THE BAKER MIGHT **WANT** TO GOUGE, BUT IF HE TRIES, OTHER BAKERS, THINKING ONLY OF THEMSELVES, WILL STEAL HIS CUSTOMERS.

BAKERY — BREAD 10 pence

BAKERY — BREAD 3 pence

EVEN IF HE'S THE ONLY BAKER IN TOWN, HE CAN'T GET TOO GREEDY. IF HE STARTS MAKING CRAZY MONEY, OTHER PEOPLE WILL DROP WHAT THEY'RE DOING AND **HORN IN**.

BAKERY — BREAD 10 pence

~~WIGMAKER~~ BAKERY — BREAD 5 pence

So in Smith's economy, **competition** kept everyone honest. Every baker—saint and greedhead alike—was led, "as if by an invisible hand," to sell bread at a fair price: high enough to pay for the baker's costs and work, low enough that others didn't steal the customers.

BAKERY — BREAD 3 pence

I WANT TO CHARGE MORE, BUT I CAN'T!

~~WIGMAKER~~ BAKERY

Speaking of costs, the baker's suppliers, workers, landlord, and lenders couldn't overcharge either, or the baker would go to their competitors. And so on.

So the price of a loaf of bread included the fair price of all the land, labor, and capital that went into it—in other words, the bread sold for its cost to society.

MORE OR LESS.

Here's the free market in *action*. Let's say there's a bad wheat harvest. The government could intervene...

IMPORT MORE WHEAT!

Shipper

YOU! RELEASE YOUR STOCKPILES!

Grain merchant

YOU! EAT LESS WHEAT!

WHEAT WHEAT WHEAT WHEAT WHEAT

Or it could do *nothing*. The price of wheat will rise, and then:

People will tighten their belts and substitute other foods.

Merchants will sell their stockpiles for a big profit.

Shippers will import more wheat to take advantage of the high price.

POTATOES AGAIN?

GOUGER! WHATEVER.

BLESS YOU!

WHATEVER.

WHEAT

WHEAT WHEAT

In other words, a *free market* organizes things, far more effectively than a human planner ever could. Imagine if a planner tried to arrange the supplies of modern New York City.

GASOLINE BEER LIGHTBULBS BLACK CLOTHES HAMMERS BAGELS ART SUPPLIES LOLLIPOPS COFFEE BRICKS BETTER COFFEE ASPIRIN

By *not* planning its supplies, New York has almost never had a short-age of anything (except space).

If buyers can't buy from whomever they want, if sellers can't set their own prices, or if wigmakers aren't allowed to become bakers, the system won't work right. So people must be left reasonably *free*.

BAKERY

BREAD 10 PENCE

WIGMAKER

So we're back to:

LAISSEZ-FAIRE!

But now we understand why:

PINS
100 FOR
A PENNY

- To **get**, people have to **give**—they have to sell something others want.

- If someone tries to charge too much, others will horn in until the price drops.

- So everything sells for roughly the cost of the land, labor, and capital it took to make the item.

IN OTHER WORDS, ITS COST TO **SOCIETY**.

If people **don't** buy a product, it means the product's not worth the cost of the resources used to make it. The seller goes out of business, freeing up the land, labor, and capital he was wasting.

NO GREAT LOSS!

LOVINGLY HANDCRAFTED PINS

1 FOR A PENNY

SO IN SMITH'S ECONOMY, THE **MARKET ITSELF** FIGURED OUT WHAT PEOPLE WANTED, AND HOW TO GET IT TO THEM MOST EFFICIENTLY, EVEN THOUGH EVERYONE **IN** THE MARKET WAS JUST TRYING TO MAKE A LIVING.

SMITH'S IDEA THAT THE MARKET CAN PROVIDE **ORDER** WITHOUT ANYONE GIVING **ORDERS** HAS BEEN THE CORE OF ECONOMIC THOUGHT EVER SINCE.

WEALTH OF NATIONS

BUT IT SOMETIMES SEEMS THAT PEOPLE SPEND MORE TIME **REVERING** ADAM SMITH THAN **READING** HIM. SMITH HAD **OTHER** THINGS TO SAY, THINGS THAT HAVE BEEN LARGELY FORGOTTEN. LET'S LOOK AT SOME OF THEM.

THE LIMITS OF THE MARKET

Adam Smith was never dogmatic; he knew markets weren't perfect. Markets won't enforce laws, protect borders, or provide **public goods**, such as street cleaning, that everyone wants but nobody has much incentive to provide.

THOSE ARE JOBS FOR *GOVERNMENT*.

For that matter, Smith thought government should favor war-related industries so they would be around if war came, protect wage workers (because they had less bargaining power than employers), keep banks honest, issue patents, protect new industries until they were on their feet, cap the interest rate, control disease, establish education standards (so brain-dead *jobs* like the ones in the pin workshop didn't turn workers into brain-dead *people*), and even provide public amusements.

"Cap the interest rate" was a big one. Smith understood that if the reward gets too big, investors forget the *risk*.

INVEST IN A FARM VERY SAFE 4% INTEREST

INVEST IN A TRADING JOURNEY TO BRAZIL RATHER RISKY, BUT 8% INTEREST

INVEST IN GOLD MINES ON THE MOON! 300% INTEREST!!!

With the interest rate capped, Smith expected people to take reasonable risks but avoid wild gambles.

FARM 4%

BRAZIL 8%

THE MOON 8%

Smith didn't just think interest should be low; he thought the same about *profit*. Smith thought that high profits were *bad*, because you couldn't have high profits and high wages at the same time.

YOUR WAGES COME OUT OF OUR PROFIT!

YOUR PROFITS COME OUT OF OUR WAGES!

High wages weren't just in workers' interest; they were in *society's* interest, because almost everyone *in* society was a worker. That's still true today: If your income comes from the work you do, and not from rent or profit, *you're* a worker.

Which brings up a point so basic that it can be hard to see.

"NO SOCIETY CAN SURELY BE FLOURISHING AND HAPPY, OF WHICH THE FAR GREATER PART OF THE MEMBERS [THE WORKERS] ARE POOR AND MISERABLE."

So when capitalists followed their self-interest and paid low wages, that was *bad* for society.

Same if they raised prices: when prices rose, *real wages*—not the money itself, but what the money would buy—fell.

HIGH PRICES AND LOW WAGES ARE THE SAME DAMN THING!

That's one reason Smith liked free markets: in a free market, capitalists compete for workers, which raises wages.

They also compete for customers, which lowers prices.

I OFFER THREE SHILLINGS A DAY!

FOUR!

YOU CAN HAVE IT FOR SIXPENCE!

FIVE!

But even back in Smith's day, *big* capitalists could *escape the market*.

For one thing, they could *take over* a market.

WILL ONE OF YOU TAKE EIGHT PENCE?

BREAD 10 p.

BREAD 10 p.

NO!

"PEOPLE OF THE SAME TRADE SELDOM MEET TOGETHER, EVEN FOR MERRIMENT AND DIVERSION, BUT THE CONVERSATION ENDS IN A CONSPIRACY AGAINST THE PUBLIC, OR IN SOME CONTRIVANCE TO RAISE PRICES."

Even worse: Big capitalists had enough political *power* to push for laws establishing *subsidies* and *protective tariffs* that guaranteed high profits.

IN A WORD, *MERCANTILISM*.

Those laws were bad for society, but who understood that? Not the tired, uneducated worker. Or for that matter, the *government*, much of the time.

WHAT'S GOOD FOR ME IS GOOD FOR *EVERYONE*!

YOU'RE THE EXPERT.

HUH?

SO ADAM SMITH DIDN'T EXACTLY THINK GOVERNMENT WAS DANGEROUS TO THE FREE MARKET. HE THOUGHT THE DANGER WAS BIG CAPITALISTS *TRICKING* GOVERNMENT INTO DOING THEM FAVORS.

Which brings us to the big *forgotten message* of The Wealth of Nations:

BEWARE OF CAPITALISTS!

It's worth reading in Adam Smith's own words.

"THE PROPOSAL OF ANY NEW LAW OR REGULATION OF COMMERCE WHICH COMES FROM [CAPITALISTS] OUGHT ALWAYS TO BE LISTENED TO WITH GREAT PRECAUTION, AND OUGHT NEVER TO BE ADOPTED, TILL AFTER HAVING BEEN LONG AND CAREFULLY EXAMINED, NOT ONLY WITH THE MOST SCRUPULOUS, BUT WITH THE MOST SUSPICIOUS ATTENTION. IT COMES FROM AN ORDER OF MEN, WHOSE INTEREST IS NEVER EXACTLY THE SAME WITH THAT OF THE PUBLIC, WHO HAVE GENERALLY AN INTEREST TO DECEIVE AND EVEN TO OPPRESS THE PUBLIC, AND WHO ACCORDINGLY HAVE, UPON MANY OCCASIONS, BOTH DECEIVED AND OPPRESSED IT."

Smith had a bit of a *problem* with big capitalists.

"THE MEAN RAPACITY, THE MONOPOLIZING SPIRIT OF MERCHANTS AND MANUFACTURERS, WHO NEITHER ARE, NOR OUGHT TO BE, THE MASTERS OF MANKIND..."

And for good reason. Britain's economy was freer than France's (Smith thought that was why Britain was richer), but it was still riddled with regulations, subsidies, protections, and especially *government-enforced monopolies*.

A *monopoly* is when there's only *one* seller in a market. With no competition, the monopolist can—and will—overcharge.

BREAD 10 pence

For instance, in Smith's day only the giant East India Company could trade with Asia.

OUR MONOPOLY *ENCOURAGES* US TO TRADE WITH ASIA!

THAT MAKES NO SENSE! IF THE ASIA TRADE PAYS, WHY KEEP PEOPLE OUT OF IT? IF IT DOESN'T, WHY ENCOURAGE IT?

The very *existence* of the East India Company was an interference in the market—the EIC was a government-created entity called a *corporation*.

THE ARTIFICIAL PERSON: The Corporation

A corporation is a *legal person*. It can enter contracts, borrow money, employ workers, go to court, own property, pay taxes, and so on.

At first, every corporation was unique, but now they've come to resemble one another.

The owners or *stockholders* contribute money for *shares* of the company's *stock* (in other words, they buy slices of the company).

Money (or *capital*)

Stock

Dividends

The corporation uses the money from the sale of stock to do business; the profit is either reinvested in the business or *divided* among the shareholders (the payout is called a *dividend*).

If a corporation fails, the stockholders can lose the money they invested, but nothing more. This is called *limited liability*.

IOU IOU IOU IOU IOU

Shareholders don't run big corporations.

They elect *directors* . . .

who direct *managers*.

ELECT

APPOINT AND SUPERVISE

THAT LETS CROWDS OF PEOPLE POOL THEIR MONEY TO UNDERTAKE BIG PROJECTS (NOT EVERY CORPORATION IS A BIG BUSINESS, BUT ALMOST EVERY BIG BUSINESS IS A CORPORATION). IT ALSO MEANS THAT BIG BUSINESS *TAKES ON A LIFE OF ITS OWN*. YOU MAY OWN STOCK IN FORD, BUT THAT GIVES YOU VERY LITTLE *POWER* OVER FORD; YOU'RE MOSTLY ALONG FOR THE RIDE.

In fact, it usually **doesn't matter** who owns the shares, which is why stocks can be bought and sold freely.

STOCK MARKET

The whole arrangement is awkward and inefficient: Managers will never work as hard for someone else's business as they would for their own.

"NEGLIGENCE AND PROFUSION, THEREFORE, MUST ALWAYS PREVAIL, MORE OR LESS, IN THE MANAGEMENT OF THE AFFAIRS OF SUCH A COMPANY."

"TO BE MERELY USELESS, INDEED, IS PERHAPS THE HIGHEST EULOGY WHICH CAN EVER JUSTLY BE BESTOWED UPON A [CORPORATION]."

In fact, in Smith's day, corporations were so cumbersome that they needed government favors just to survive. To Smith, one benefit of laissez-faire was that it would **kill** these corporations.

DOWN WITH THE MAN!

Corporations weren't the only ones to get favors. For instance, English merchants had legal monopolies on trade with England's American colonies.

That meant high profits for English merchants, but English and American consumers paid higher prices **and** higher taxes to enforce the law.

"THE SNEAKING ARTS OF . . . TRADESMEN ARE THUS ERECTED INTO POLITICAL MAXIMS FOR THE CONDUCT OF A GREAT EMPIRE."

Another consequence: **The American Revolution.**

LIBERTY OR DEATH: The American Revolution

It's well known that British *taxes* irritated the American colonists.

TAXATION WITHOUT REPRESENTATION IS TYRANNY!

But those British *monopolies* upset them, too.

Even the East India Company annoyed the colonists. It overcharged . . .

IT WOULD BE CHEAPER TO GO TO CHINA AND BUY TEA MYSELF!

NOT ALLOWED!

E.I.C.

TEA £10

and when the company nearly collapsed, through its own shortsighted greed, the British government rescued it with a *tax break*, while the *colonists* still paid a tax on tea.

The colonists felt better after dumping the EIC's tea in the drink (the Boston Tea Party, 1773).

DOWN WITH CORPORATIONS!

TEA

The Boston Tea Party helped set the American Revolution (1775-1783) in motion; soon France—in the habit of fighting England since page 18—joined in on the American side.

THE ENEMY OF MY ENEMY IS MY FRIEND!

By the time Britain lost, the cost of the war had sent the French debt *out of control*.

IOU IOU IOU IOU IOU IOU

French economists saw the *crisis* as an *opportunity*.

LOUIS XVI

NOW'S THE CHANCE TO MAKE OUR *WHOLE ECONOMY* WORK LIKE IT SHOULD.

To impose radical changes, King Louis XVI needed the approval of the *Estates-General*, France's parliament. The Estates-General hadn't met in more than a century, so a bunch of brand-new delegates showed up, afire with radical ideas.

LIKE WHAT?

LIKE *WE'RE* THE GOVERNMENT!

VIVE LA REVOLUTION, CITIZEN!

THE BEST OF TIMES, QUICKLY FOLLOWED BY THE WORST OF TIMES:
The French Revolution

The Estates-General renamed itself the **National Assembly** and set to work fixing everything.

> IF WE REMOVE IRRATIONAL LAWS, SUPERSTITIONS, AND TRADE BARRIERS, PEOPLE WILL BE GUIDED BY THEIR **NATURAL REASON!**

But people didn't suddenly become rational. Taxpayers didn't pay their rational taxes.... The price of bread kept spiking.... The National Assembly split into factions.

> THE FIRST **LEFTISTS** AND **RIGHTISTS!**

RADICALS, ON THE SPEAKER'S LEFT

CONSERVATIVES (RELATIVELY SPEAKING), ON THE SPEAKER'S RIGHT

The Left went nuts and killed their rivals in a **reign of terror**.

Chaos, invasions, the military rule of Napoleon Bonaparte, and two decades of war followed.

The collapse of the French Revolution's lofty hopes disillusioned a generation. European writers wrote of **progress** leading to **horror** . . .

> WE'VE CREATED A MONSTER!

Frankenstein, Published in 1818

and not just novelists. The champion pessimist of the age, maybe of all time, was the British scholar **Thomas Malthus** (1766-1834).

THE SCIENTISTS: Malthus and Ricardo

Malthus's *An Essay on the Principle of Population* (1798) was clear and logical:

Left to itself, the population **doubles** every few decades—a **geometrical** increase.

But once all the good land is in use, the food supply can't grow at the same rate. At best, we can hope for an **arithmetical** increase.

The inevitable result: **starvation**.

Progress, like ending disease and war, only makes things *worse*. Disease and war keep the population in balance with the food supply.

PROGRESS STINKS!

Even *charity* is a bad idea—feed the starving today, and you'll have *more* people starving tomorrow.

SORRY!

MALTHUS WAS RIGHT THAT WE CAN'T HAVE INFINITE POPULATION GROWTH ON A FINITE PLANET. OR INFINITE ECONOMIC GROWTH, FOR THAT MATTER.

But Malthus, a parson, downplayed *birth control*, even though some people used it back then.

WE JUST DON'T *TALK* ABOUT IT.

The very poor *didn't* use birth control. They lacked the money to buy it and the education to understand what worked.

DON'T WORRY, BABY. I'M WEARING AN AMULET.

Plus, poor people *needed* many children to make sure some survived to support them in their old age.

THEY'RE OUR RETIREMENT PLAN!

So people weren't just poor because they bred; they bred because they were poor.

WE'RE BAREFOOT BECAUSE WE'RE PREGNANT!

WE'RE PREGNANT BECAUSE WE'RE BAREFOOT!

Still, Malthus's ideas caught on, especially with the rich.

PLEASE, SIR, I'M STARVING...

YOUR PROBLEM IS YOU HAVE *TOO MUCH SEX!*

Malthus, by the way, is part of the reason economics came to be called the *dismal science*.

THE "DISMAL" PART. IN CASE THAT WASN'T CLEAR.

The "science" part came from Malthus's friend, the English economist *David Ricardo* (1772-1823).

Possibly the most important person nobody's ever heard of.

David Ricardo's *Principles of Political Economy and Taxation* (1817) is just what the title says: a collection of logical, consistent, abstract *principles*.

Abstraction involves *simplification*. For instance, Ricardo simplified *money*. To Ricardo, things exchanged for things, in proportion to the labor they took to make. So a purchase of an axe (or anything else) was really just an exchange of labor for labor.

1 hour of an iron miner's labor

1 hour of a coal miner's labor

1 hour of a blacksmith's labor (which counts as 2 hours because of the time it took to train the blacksmith)

1/4 hour of a carter's labor in taking it to market

SELLS FOR

The *labor theory of value* (really, the labor theory of *price*)

The amount of gold that takes 4 1/4 hours to mine and mint into coins

Ricardo also simplified *people*. His principles operated on *economic man*, who thinks about his own gain and nothing else.

MORE... MORE... MORE...

The result of these and other simplifications was an entire *abstract economy*—a collection of *idealized models* of Adam Smith's free market.

BAKERY BREAD 10 P.

BAKERY BREAD 5 P.

SIMPLIFIED DOESN'T NECESSARILY MEAN *SIMPLE*. ONE OF RICARDO'S MODELS, CALLED *COMPARATIVE ADVANTAGE*, IS THE HAIRIEST CONCEPT WE'LL COVER IN THIS BOOK. LET'S CHECK IT OUT.

In this model, Ricardo **excluded** all countries except England and Portugal, and all products except wine and clothes.

Obviously, if each country makes one thing more efficiently, it makes sense to specialize and **trade**.

YOU MAKE WINE; WE'LL MAKE CLOTHES!

1 worker makes 2 casks of wine or 4 bundles of clothes per year.

1 worker makes 4 casks of wine or 2 bundles of clothes per year.

Now let's imagine England is just plain **inefficient**. Does trade still make sense? Common sense says **no**.

WE'RE AT A **DISADVANTAGE** HERE. IF WE LET YOUR CHEAP GOODS IN, THEY'D SWAMP US!

WHY WOULD WE **TRADE** FOR THINGS WE CAN **MAKE** FASTER?

1 worker makes 2 casks of wine or 4 bundles of clothes per year.

1 worker makes 4 casks of wine or 6 bundles of clothes per year.

BUT WAIT: IF ENGLAND SWITCHES, SAY, 100 WORKERS FROM MAKING WINE TO MAKING CLOTHES, YOU'LL MAKE 200 FEWER CASKS OF WINE BUT 400 MORE BUNDLES OF CLOTHES. SEND PORTUGAL 380 BUNDLES AND YOU'LL STILL HAVE 20 **MORE** THAN YOU STARTED WITH.

RIGHT.... SO?

THEN IF **PORTUGAL** SWITCHES 60 WORKERS FROM CLOTHES TO WINE, YOU'LL MAKE 360 **FEWER** BUNDLES OF CLOTHES, BUT THAT'S OK BECAUSE THE ENGLISH ARE SENDING YOU 380.

OK...

AND THE 60 WORKERS WILL MAKE 240 **MORE** CASKS OF WINE. SEND 220 CASKS TO ENGLAND, AND EVERYONE HAS MORE STUFF THAN THEY STARTED WITH!

ENGLAND / -200 WINE / +400 CLOTHES
+220 FROM P / -380 TO P
+20 / +20

PORTUGAL / +240 WINE / -360 CLOTHES
-220 TO E / +380 FROM E
+20 / +20

IT DOES SEEM TO WORK...

CREEPY!

Don't worry if you didn't get that on first read. The point is that a **simplified model** of international trade gave us an insight that we might not have reached by observation alone: A country, **even one at a disadvantage**, can profit from free trade by specializing where it has **less** of a disadvantage.

A COMPARATIVE ADVANTAGE!

Almost immediately, David Ricardo's abstract approach, called **classical political economy**, took over economic thought.

IT'S **SCIENCE**!

Adam Smith is often called a classical economist, but really he was very different; his rich tapestry of real butchers and bakers making real decisions didn't much resemble the abstract, theoretical world of classical political economy.

Classical political economy was well suited for classrooms, and in the early 19th century, the mainstream of economic thought moved to **academia**. We'll be drawing mainstream economists like **this** from now on:

Even today, most of economics is a product of academia, and most economists think in terms of exact, rigorous models.

SCIENCE!

FEARSOMELY COMPLEX MATH

But let's take another look at comparative advantage. Here are some real-world possibilities Ricardo simply **excluded** from his model to keep it simple.

WHAT'S TO STOP BRITISH BOSSES FROM MOVING THEIR OPERATIONS TO EFFICIENT PORTUGAL, LEAVING BRITISH WORKERS WITHOUT JOBS? WHAT IF THE EFFORT OF **SHIPPING** ALL THAT STUFF IS MORE THAN THE GAIN FROM TRADE? AND WHAT IF TRADE **BREAKS DOWN**? PORTUGAL WILL HAVE **ALL** THE WINE AND **NO** CLOTHES!

WHAT'S YOUR POINT?

The comparative advantage model **may** work in the real world, but it also may **not**. By itself, a model doesn't **prove** anything.

But Ricardo's models were so **compelling** that people kept **forgetting** that, no matter how often economists tried to remind them.

"GREAT IS THE USEFULNESS OF RICARDO'S METHOD. BUT EVEN GREATER ARE THE EVILS WHICH MAY ARISE FROM A CRUDE APPLICATION OF ITS SUGGESTIONS TO REAL PROBLEMS. FOR THAT SIMPLICITY WHICH MAKES IT HELPFUL, ALSO MAKES IT DEFICIENT AND TREACHEROUS."

Alfred Marshall (1842-1924), British economist

And people still **keep right on** forgetting. We still hear things like **this**:

FREE TRADE IS **ALWAYS** A GOOD IDEA! COMPARATIVE ADVANTAGE **PROVES** IT!

The bourgeoisie, during its rule of scarce one hundred years, has created more massive and more colossal productive forces than have all preceding generations together. Subjection of nature's forces to man, machinery, application of chemistry to industry and agriculture, steam-navigation, railways, electric telegraphs, clearing of whole continents for cultivation, canalization of rivers, whole populations conjured out of the ground – what earlier century had even a presentiment that such productive forces slumbered in the lap of social labour?

—Karl Marx and Friedrich Engels,
The Communist Manifesto (1848)

For that matter, when we hear people say *this* . . .

THE FREE MARKET *ALWAYS* WORKS! LAISSEZ-FAIRE!

they're not describing the real world. They're describing Ricardo-style *abstract models*.

Step 1: Assume an idealized free market.

Step 2: Perform calculations based on that assumption.

Step 3: Your calculations will show that the free market is ideal.

Which is not entirely coincidence—it works nicely for the rich and powerful.

One reason: A model free market functions like a finely tuned machine, assigning people an income based on how much they do for others. So in a textbook-perfect free market, if you're rich, it's because you *deserve* to be.

HOW ABOUT WE TAX YOU AND SPEND THE MONEY ON ME?

THAT WOULD BE LIKE THROWING A WRENCH INTO THE MACHINE. WE'D *ALL* WIND UP WORSE OFF.

The idea that *things are as they ought to be* is always comforting, and people *needed* to be comforted in the early 19th century: The *real* economy was going through wrenching, confusing shifts.

THE INDUSTRIAL REVOLUTION WAS CHANGING EVERYTHING!

PRINCIPLES

CHOOF CHOOF CHOOF

41

CHAPTER 2

FULL STEAM AHEAD

AHEAD

(1820–1865)

The revolutionary part of the Industrial Revolution? **Steam power**.

STEAM PUSHES.

FIRE TURNS WATER TO STEAM.

To understand steam, we have to look at:

COAL

Coal, like oil, is a fossil fuel.

IT'S DINOSAUR MEAT!

Britain has lots of coal; Britons used cheap coal instead of expensive firewood as early as the Middle Ages.

COAL

BUY COAL! SAVE THE TREES!

5p. a bag

But coal mines flood, and until 1700 or so there was only one reliable source of power for **pumping**, the same one there had been since forever: **muscle**.

AND THE EXTRA WORKERS ARE *EXPENSIVE*.

Then in 1704, Thomas Newcomen, an English ironmonger, developed an "atmospheric engine" (an early steam engine) and rigged it to pump out a coal mine. Fire replaced muscle.

DO YOU REALIZE WE'RE PRESENT AT THE BIRTH OF THE MODERN WORLD?

HUH?

But Newcomen's engine *devoured* fuel; it cost more to run than regular old human-powered pumps except where fuel was very *cheap* (like in a coal mine). So not much more happened for decades.

In the 1760s, the Scottish engineer James Watt designed efficient engines that paid their way just about anywhere. Soon entrepreneurs hitched them up to weaving and spinning machines and *factories* sprang up, churning out tons of stuff (mostly cotton cloth at first).

Steam engines were soon *helping* move goods to the customers, via the *steamship* (1807)...

and *railroad* (1820s).

BRITAIN STARTED CHANGING... *FAST!*

45

SLUMPS WERE PRETTY WEIRD: HOW COULD THERE BE *TOO MUCH STUFF*?

CLOTH

The problem wasn't that people didn't *want* stuff. People usually want more stuff.

UNLESS THEY'RE BUDDHISTS.

They just didn't have the *money* to buy what they wanted. Factories can double or triple the amount of goods they produce, but not the amount of money in the economy.

CLOTH

The government wouldn't just print more money. The 19th century was the great age of the *gold standard*: Paper money could be freely cashed in for gold.

The gold standard seemed sensible; after all, paper money started out in the Middle Ages as a *receipt* for gold stored in a vault.

Really, paper money *didn't* get its value from gold. People accepted paper for the same reason that they accepted other forms of money, *including* gold: the confidence that other people would accept it.

I WANT TO TRADE MY MONEY FOR *GROCERIES*, NOT GOLD.

The gold standard bound the supply of paper money to the supply of gold, whether or not more money was needed. But there's another way to create money, even if you're on a gold standard. Let's check out *fractional reserve banking*.

Fractional reserve banking sounds exotic, but it's just the type of banking we're familiar with. Customers deposit their money...

DEPOSITS

and the bank lends it out, making money from the interest it charges.

LOANS

The bank doesn't lend all the money. It keeps a *fraction* in reserve—let's say 1/5 (20%)—and lends the rest.

So, in the 19th century, if someone deposited £1,000 at a bank...

BANK

the bank might keep 20% and lend the remaining £800 to someone else...

who would buy a steam engine with it.

who would immediately open a bank account with it.

The bank would keep 20% of that (£160) in reserve and lend the remaining £640 to someone else...

BANK

The seller would deposit the money in his bank (which might or might not be the same bank—it doesn't matter).

And so on.

If the banks kept lending the money out, and the money kept coming back, the original £1,000 would create £4,000 in extra bank accounts (£5,000 total).

£800
+ £640
+ £512 (80% of 640)
and so on, all the way down to a penny
= £4,000

That £5,000 worth of bank accounts would be backed up by £1,000 in cash and £4,000 in IOUs from the banks' borrowers.

I.O.U.

£1000

Since people could get their money from the bank whenever they wanted—or write a check and let someone else get the money—the bank accounts worked like *cash*. So banks took £1,000 in cash and turned it into £5,000 in cash.

They did that by turning *debt* into *money*. The very thought of that makes some people see red, but I'm not sure why—really, money *is* debt.

AN IOU FROM THE REST OF THE WORLD, EXCHANGEABLE FOR WORK OR GOODS

I.O.U. £4000

£1000

FRACTIONAL RESERVE BANKING STILL WORKS TODAY; IT WORKS BECAUSE WE DON'T ALL WITHDRAW OUR MONEY AT ONCE. THE FRACTION IN THE BANK'S VAULTS IS ENOUGH TO COVER WITHDRAWALS ON ANY GIVEN DAY.

INSTEAD, WE MOSTLY WRITE CHECKS TO ONE ANOTHER, OR SEND PAYMENTS ELECTRONICALLY, TRANSFERRING *OWNERSHIP* OF THE MONEY WHILE IT STAYS IN THE BANK.

BUT IN THE 19TH CENTURY, A RUMOR—TRUE OR FALSE—THAT A BANK WAS IN TROUBLE COULD START A *RUN* ON THE BANK . . .

BANK

WHERE'S MY MONEY?

WHERE?

WHERE?

IT'S OUT MAKING *MORE* MONEY.

which is why many *slumps* were set off by *panics*.

BUY SOME CLOTH?

LOVE TO, BUT MY MONEY VANISHED.

Some people thought slumps were *entirely* due to financial hiccups like bank runs.

SHARE AND SHARE ALIKE: Socialism

Some people got the idea that Adam Smith's free competition wasn't working like it was supposed to.

WHY BUILD FACTORIES JUST TO LET THEM LIE IDLE HALF THE TIME?

WHY WORK SOME WORKERS TO DEATH WHILE OTHERS STARVE FOR LACK OF A JOB?

HELP?!

IF CLOTHES ARE SO CHEAP, WHY ARE THE WORKERS WHO MAKE THEM WEARING RAGS?

ALL THIS WEALTH COULD BENEFIT *EVERYONE*! WE JUST HAVE TO *COOPERATE*!

WHAT SHOULD WE CALL OURSELVES?

COLLECTIVISTS?

NAAH.

ANTI-INDIVIDUALISTS?

BARF.

SOCIALISTS?

THAT WORKS.

But while cooperating *sounded* easy...

I HAVE THE PERFECT PLAN. LET'S GET TO WORK!

AHEM. *MY* PLAN IS CLEARLY SUPERIOR.

DELUDED FOOLS! ONLY *MY* IDEAS WILL WORK!

socialists' arguments went on and on because they were never put to the test of experience.

MORON!

CRETIN! HAVEN'T YOU READ FEUERBACH'S COMMENTARIES ON HEGEL?

"I ALONE HAVE CONFOUNDED TWENTY CENTURIES OF POLITICAL IMBECILITY: AND IT IS TO ME ALONE THAT PRESENT AND FUTURE GENERATIONS WILL LOOK FOR THE ORIGIN OF THEIR IMMENSE HAPPINESS!" —CHARLES FOURIER, (1772-1837), FRENCH SOCIALIST PHILOSOPHER

One socialist did get his hands dirty: *Friedrich Engels* (1820-1895).

Engels traveled from Germany, where his father owned a factory, to **Manchester**, center of the British cloth industry and the world's first great industrial city.

While he was there, Engels explored the **slums**, emerging with *The Condition of the Working Class in England in 1844*. His conclusion:

IT'S *BAD!*

And 1844 was a **boom** year. Engels predicted another **crash** in 1847 . . .

1800 1805 1810 1815 1820 1825 1830 1835 1840 1845

= SLUMPS

and that soon a crash would spark a **revolution**.

"ONE CAN VERY NEARLY FIX THE DATE...."

The crash came on schedule; in 1848, revolutions followed all over Europe, except in England, which came close.

That same year, Engels and a German philosopher, Karl Marx (1818-1883), published the *Manifesto of the Communist Party*. (At the time, *communist* was another term for *socialist*.)

HOW MANY MEMBERS IN THE COMMUNIST PARTY?

BOTH OF US!

The *Communist Manifesto* is short and clear, but it contains a whole theory of history—the idea that history is really about *class struggle*.

In this view, the *bourgeoisie* (capitalists) destroyed agrarian society, and good riddance.

But the bourgeoisie were grabbing *all* the capital, while everyone else was sinking into the *proletariat*—the destitute masses.

"YOU ARE HORRIFIED BY OUR INTENDING TO DO AWAY WITH PRIVATE PROPERTY. BUT IN YOUR EXISTING SOCIETY, PRIVATE PROPERTY IS ALREADY DONE AWAY WITH FOR NINE-TENTHS OF THE POPULATION. . . ."

The good news: When everyone's a prole, they'll be *united*, while the bourgeoisie drive each other out of business until only a few remain.

Then . . .

At which point the proles (that is, everyone) will somehow run the factories for the good of all.

WORKERS OF THE WORLD, UNITE!

But the workers didn't unite, and most of the 1848 revolutions failed. Marx fled to England with a mission:

I'LL *PROVE* THE REVOLUTION'S COMING! SEE IF I DON'T!

Marx spent two decades working on his proof, so let's leave him for now.

SKRITCH SKRITCH SKRITCH

ON THE OTHER HAND: The Benefits of Industry

WE'VE SPENT A LOT OF TIME ON THE DARK SIDE OF THE INDUSTRIAL REVOLUTION; LET'S TAKE ANOTHER LOOK AT THE *BRIGHT* SIDE.

For one thing, the business cycle was more up than down, if you stepped back.

YOU JUST HAVE TO LOOK AT THE *LONG RUN!*

Plus, factory products did reach the poor. Before the Industrial Revolution, most people just *did without* all sorts of things we take for granted.

MASS PRO-DUCTION MEANS PRO-DUCTION FOR THE MASSES!

And as hard as life was in the factories, it was often worse on the farm, where little had changed since forever.

French farmer painted around 1415

French farmer painted around 1850

For instance, in agricultural Ireland, a million people (*one in eight* Irish) starved to death between 1845 and 1849 in the *potato famine*.

Industrial poverty was more *visible* than rural poverty, but wasn't necessarily harsher.

WE COULD GO BACK TO THE FARM.

ARE YOU CRAZY?

ALSO, WHEN TIMES GOT TOUGH, DESPERATE PEOPLE COULD SOMETIMES *LEAVE*. LET'S FOLLOW SOME TO THE YOUNG *UNITED STATES OF AMERICA*.

DEMOCRACY IN AMERICA

The United States, which we last saw at the end of the American Revolution, had a shaky start. The first government, the **Continental Congress**, had no power to **tax**. That stopped it from becoming a dictatorship; it also stopped it from doing much else.

IT APPEARS REPRESENTATION WITHOUT TAXATION IS POINTLESS. . . .

The **Constitution** (1789) gave the government more power. Alexander Hamilton, secretary of the Treasury, wanted people with money to wield this new power; Secretary of State Thomas Jefferson imagined a democracy.

Hamilton

"THE PEOPLE WHO OWN THE COUNTRY OUGHT TO GOVERN IT."

Jefferson

John Jay

"I KNOW OF NO SAFE DEPOSITORY OF THE POWERS OF THE SOCIETY BUT THE PEOPLE THEMSELVES. . . ."

Jefferson was a slaveowner, but he didn't think like one. He understood that people who want to be **politically** independent should be **economically** independent. To him that meant every family farming its own land.

EVERY FAMILY?

IN THEORY!

JEFFERSON AND HAMILTON FORMED **POLITICAL PARTIES.** HAMILTON'S FEDERALISTS ARE LONG GONE, BUT JEFFERSON'S DEMOCRATS ARE STILL WITH US.

Jefferson became president in 1800, and in 1804 Vice President Aaron Burr shot Hamilton in a duel, so the early republic was **Jeffersonian**, with cheap land for settlers.

Cheap land meant workers had **bargaining power.**

GIMME A RAISE OR I'LL GRAB A FARM!

W • E

Thing is, well-paid workers do better work than ones driven by fear and want, to the point that it's efficient to pay workers more than the minimum. Just ask Adam Smith.

"WHERE WAGES ARE HIGH...WE SHALL ALWAYS FIND THE WORKMEN MORE ACTIVE, DILIGENT, AND EXPEDITIOUS, THAN WHERE THEY ARE LOW...." – ADAM SMITH

High wages also gave American bosses incentive to use labor more efficiently—for instance, by assembling *identical, interchangeable parts* instead of making every product as a one-off.

By the 1830s, American manufacturers and shippers could compete with British ones, not *despite* the high wages they paid American workers, but *because* of them.

With so much opportunity, Americans were expected to take care of themselves.

ANYONE WHO WORKS HARD AND STAYS SOBER CAN MAKE IT!

At least, all that was true of the North.

Down South, not so much.

Southerners blamed their problems on tariffs, taxes, bankers....They somehow *missed* a big reason:

NO SLAVERY

SLAVERY

SLAVES IN THE LAND OF THE FREE

SLAVERY IS WHAT HAPPENS WHEN YOU TAKE PROPERTY RIGHTS TOO FAR AND LET PEOPLE OWN *OTHER* PEOPLE.

Slave labor *isn't* efficient. Fear of punishment can make someone work, but not work *well*. Or as Adam Smith put it:

"THE WORK DONE BY SLAVES, THOUGH IT APPEARS TO COST ONLY THEIR MAINTENANCE, IS IN THE END THE DEAREST OF ANY."

Adam Smith

The framers of the Constitution hoped slavery would fade away. Then the cotton gin (1790s) sped up the cleaning of cotton by a hundred times, just as factories started demanding lots of cotton.

NOW COTTON'S SO PROFITABLE THAT IT CAN CARRY A SLAVE ECONOMY!

The more profitable slavery became, the less slaveowners could see wrong with it.

BLACKS ARE *SUITED* TO BE SLAVES. THEY'RE LIKE ANIMALS!

They even wanted to *spread* slavery to the rest of the country. Free workers and farmers didn't like that; they formed a new party, the Republicans.

KEEP OUR STATE FREE

DON'T LET SLAVERY SPREAD

In 1860, the Republican Abraham Lincoln won the presidency.

IT'S A VICTORY FOR THE LITTLE GUY!

THE FREAKISHLY TALL LITTLE GUY!

The South *seceded*, then *attacked*, and the Civil War was on.

59

THE WAR BETWEEN THE ECONOMIES

It takes more than cotton to fight a war, so the South had trouble even keeping its army in the field.

The North just printed money and bought what it needed.

Northern businesses did great, partly cheating the government.

A. Carnegie

J.P.

"YOU CAN SELL ANYTHING TO THE GOVERNMENT AT ALMOST ANY PRICE IF YOU'VE GOT THE GUTS TO ASK." - JAMES "DIAMOND JIM" FISK (1835-1872), BUSINESSMAN

Businesses provided Union troops with dud powder, maggoty meat, shells that exploded at inconvenient times, and uniforms made of **shoddy**—glued lint that dissolved in the rain.

TRADE YOU SOME COFFEE FOR SOME GUNPOWDER?

THE NORTH FINALLY WON THE CIVIL WAR IN 1865, WHICH IS A GOOD POINT TO CATCH OUR BREATH.

Colbert becomes finance minister

Watt's engine

Malthus's *Essay*

Communist Manifesto

Economic Table

French Revolution

First passenger railroad

1665   1759 1765   1789   1798   1821   1848   1861–
1672   1704   1776   1807   1817   1860   1865

Dutch eat prime minister

Wealth of Nations

First passenger steamboat

Lincoln elected

Newcomen's engine

American Revolution

Ricardo's *Principles*

Civil War

Let's pick up the story with Karl Marx, back in England.

SCRITCH SCRITCH SCRITCH

THE ANGRY ECONOMIST: Marx and *Capital*

In 1867, Marx finished the fearsome *Das Kapital* (*Capital* in English).

VOLUME 1!

Marx, remember, wanted to **prove** that revolution was coming. To him, that meant proving it in **economists' own terms.** Marx had read just about **every** economist . . .

and wasn't impressed.

"DWARF ECONOMIST!"

"PRETENTIOUS CRETINISM!"

"TWADDLE!"

"INSIPID NONSENSE!"

"SPURIOUS ERUDITION!"

"ATROCIOUS LACK OF THE CRITICAL FACULTY!"

"A GENIUS IN THE WAY OF BOURGEOIS STUPIDITY!"

WUMP

Marx kept Ricardo's *labor theory of value* (page 37), but did ask:

IF EVERYTHING SELLS FOR ITS LABOR COST, WHERE DOES **PROFIT** COME FROM?

His answer? *Labor itself.*

THE CAPITALIST HIRES THE WORKER FOR HIS **COST**, ENOUGH WEALTH TO KEEP THE WORKER ALIVE.

BUT THE DAY IS LONG, AND THE WORKER IS STRONG. HE MAKES **MUCH MORE WEALTH** THAN WHAT'S NEEDED TO KEEP HIM ALIVE. THAT **SURPLUS VALUE** IS THE CAPITALIST'S PROFIT.

MARKET

NOW FOLLOW THE LOGIC: AS MACHINES IMPROVE, FACTORIES NEED FEWER WORKERS . . .

BUT PROFIT COMES FROM **SQUEEZING** WORKERS. FEWER WORKERS TO SQUEEZE MEANS **LESS PROFIT.** EVENTUALLY WE WIND UP WITH AN ARMY OF UNEMPLOYED AND A FEW CAPITALISTS WHO CAN'T MAKE A PROFIT.

So we're back to the *Communist Manifesto. Capital* was the *Manifesto* redone as classical political economy.

OCEANS OF INK HAVE BEEN SPILLED TRYING TO SUPPORT OR DISPROVE MARX'S LOGIC.

BUT MARX'S LOGIC APPLIED TO RICARDO'S MODEL ECONOMY, AND WE DON'T LIVE IN THAT MODEL.

Capital did make lots of good real-world points, like: "Labor" is *people*, not just another commodity.

And a big one: *Mass production* needs *mass organization*—more than Smith's free market can handle. So big industries will be run by *someone*, who may as well be *us*—in other words, the economy will socialize itself.

IT'S AUTOMATIC!

Another big insight: Capitalists, as a group, can't make a profit if they don't employ anyone.

Capitalists will pay workers as little as possible...

Which leads us (though not necessarily Marx) to a big *problem* with capitalism:

but they need consumers to have money.

GOODS

MARKET

That's a problem because most consumers *are* workers.

?

GOODS

Where will their spending money come from?

Marx's biggest insight in *Capital*: *Industrial* capitalism was just plain different from Smith's *market* capitalism, and needed to be understood on its own terms.

PINS ≠ PINCORP.

But *Capital's* good points can get lost in tangled logic and impossible prose. It's hard to imagine workers reading *Capital* on their lunch break.

"IN THE VELOCITY OF CIRCULATION, THEREFORE, THERE APPEARS THE FLUID UNITY OF THE ANTITHETICAL AND COMPLEMENTARY PHASES, I.E. THE TRANSFORMATION OF THE COMMODITIES FROM THE FORM OF UTILITY INTO THE FORM OF VALUE AND THEIR RE-TRANSFORMATION IN THE REVERSE DIRECTION, OR THE TWO PROCESSES OF SALE AND PURCHASE."

CAPITAL CAPITAL

NOT EXACTLY "WORKERS OF THE WORLD UNITE," IS IT?

That didn't mean workers were passive. In Britain, they were *unionizing*.

UNIONS (AND REFORM)

In a union, the workers bargain as a *unit* instead of bidding one another down.

SEVEN SHILLINGS A WEEK!

WE WON'T TAKE THAT!

DAMN STRAIGHT!

I WI— OW!

THIS *COLLECTIVE BARGAINING* RESTORES THE WORKERS' BARGAINING POWER.

IT'S UNFAIR! I DON'T GET A UNION!

YOU'RE ALREADY A UNIT.

By the second half of the 19th century, unions were winning fights here and there.

FINE, NINE SHILLINGS A WEEK.

HURRAH!

More good news for workers: The British government stopped treating factory conditions as a private matter and started intervening, like with the *Factory Act of 1850*, which capped the workweek at "only" 60 hours.

Also, the *cooperative* movement experimented with having banks, mines, and other businesses run *collectively*.

WHO'S THE BOSS?

WE ARE!

Cooperatives worked OK; some people thought it would be an easy jump to a collective *society*. But we cooperate much better in small groups than in big ones.

WE *EVOLVED* TO LIVE IN SMALL, COOPERATIVE GROUPS!

By the time *Capital* was published, workers' lives were finally improving, thanks to **gradual reform**. Even Engels thought so, although he wasn't happy about it:

"THE ENGLISH PROLETARIAT IS ACTUALLY BECOMING MORE AND MORE BOURGEOIS...."

Engels wasn't happy because Marxists like him saw reform as a **distraction**. Socialists, never unified to begin with, split into:

Reformers (*socialists*)

YOU'RE NOT THE ONLY ONE WHO SEES THAT THINGS HAVE TO CHANGE!

And revolutionaries (*communists*)

THE POINT IS TO **REPLACE** CAPITALISM, NOT IMPROVE IT!

(Before the split, **communist** and **socialist** were synonyms.)

Still, Marx still expected the **people** to stage the revolution.

HEY! IF THE REVOLUTION'S **INEVITABLE**, WHO NEEDS COMMUNISTS?

Russian Marxist Vladimir Lenin (1870-1924) went further: He said communists should take power **themselves**.

THEN WE'LL HAND POWER TO THE PEOPLE! TRUST US!

However, the Russian police state had no patience for revolutionaries, or even reformers.

TO EXILE

One might have expected Germany, unified in 1871 under the "Iron Chancellor," Otto von Bismarck, to do like Russia; Bismarck was no democrat.

SOCIALISM NOW!

But to *beat* socialists, Bismarck *joined* them.

SOCIALISM NOW!

Soon German industrial workers had old-age pensions, accident insurance, and health insurance.

NOW GET TO WORK!

Big capitalists knew who was boss, too.

WE NEED A CANAL HERE.

YESSIR.

AND A SHIPYARD HERE.

YESSIR.

AND FINANCING FOR THEM.

YESSIR.

NORTH SEA

BALTIC SEA

GERMAN EMPIRE

Funding = providing money for a project.

Financing = arranging funding for a project.

By guiding key sections of the economy, while leaving others alone, Bismarck had invented the modern *mixed economy*.

CONTROLLED

Heavy industry
Industrial labor
Transport

NOT CONTROLLED

Farms
Small business

Germany's mixed economy worked— Germany started catching up to Britain. In fact, mixed economies work so well that today, pretty much every economy is a mixed economy, including the U.S. economy.

That's right—we live in a **mixed economy**, not in pure capitalism. For instance, let's take another look at modern New York. We saw on page 24 how trying to control **everything** wouldn't work...

but many things **are** controlled.

Even "free-market" goods have to meet government **quality standards**, and they're shipped in on publicly operated roads, bridges, and tunnels.

Water is a public service.

Police and **firefighters** are paid by the government.

Electricity is supplied by a tightly regulated company.

And if New York left **sanitation** and **sewage** to the market, it would soon drown in its own filth.

WE TAKE THESE THINGS FOR GRANTED, BUT MANY OF THEM STARTED AS **SOCIALIST EXPERIMENTS**. TODAY, THE QUESTION ISN'T **WHETHER** SOME PARTS OF THE ECONOMY SHOULD BE CONTROLLED BY THE PUBLIC— THE REAL QUESTIONS ARE **WHICH** PARTS, **HOW** THEY SHOULD BE CONTROLLED, AND **TO WHAT PURPOSE**.

We rarely frame the questions this way, maybe because we've become so very good at thinking in terms of **free markets**. In fact, in the late 19th century, even as the Germans experimented with socialism and the British were at least dipping a toe in the water, economists were coming up with a **new way** to think about how markets work.

SUPPLY AND DEMAND: Neoclassical Economics

Let's note one more thing about Marx's *Capital*: It was a **challenge** to mainstream economists.

YOU BELIEVE THE LABOR THEORY OF VALUE, SO YOU HAVE TO BELIEVE ME!

But soon after *Capital* came out, economists started moving **away** from Ricardo's labor theory of value.

HEY!

Léon Walras (1834–1910), French economist

Alfred Marshall (Remember him from page 40?)

William Stanley Jevons (1835–1882), British economist

They had good reason: Labor theory is **crude**. It assumes that things sell for their **average** cost. But remember Malthus's point—food won't increase as fast as population?

Another way to look at this is that every added farmer makes more food, but not **proportionally** more.

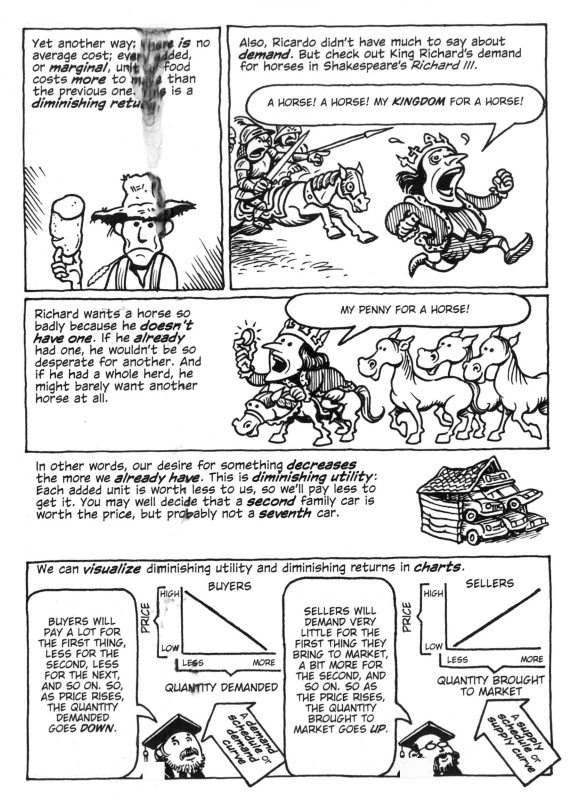

Yet another way: There *is* no average cost; ever added, or *marginal*, unit of food costs *more* to make than the previous one. This is a *diminishing returns.*

Also, Ricardo didn't have much to say about *demand*. But check out King Richard's demand for horses in Shakespeare's *Richard III*.

A HORSE! A HORSE! MY *KINGDOM* FOR A HORSE!

Richard wants a horse so badly because he *doesn't have one*. If he *already* had one, he wouldn't be so desperate for another. And if he had a whole herd, he might barely want another horse at all.

MY PENNY FOR A HORSE!

In other words, our desire for something *decreases* the more we *already have*. This is *diminishing utility*: Each added unit is worth less to us, so we'll pay less to get it. You may well decide that a *second* family car is worth the price, but probably not a *seventh* car.

We can *visualize* diminishing utility and diminishing returns in *charts*.

BUYERS

PRICE — HIGH / LOW

LESS / MORE

QUANTITY DEMANDED

BUYERS WILL PAY A LOT FOR THE FIRST THING, LESS FOR THE SECOND, LESS FOR THE NEXT, AND SO ON. SO, AS PRICE RISES, THE QUANTITY DEMANDED GOES *DOWN*.

A demand schedule or demand curve

SELLERS WILL DEMAND VERY LITTLE FOR THE FIRST THING THEY BRING TO MARKET, A BIT MORE FOR THE SECOND, AND SO ON. SO AS THE PRICE RISES, THE QUANTITY BROUGHT TO MARKET GOES *UP*.

SELLERS

PRICE — HIGH / LOW

LESS / MORE

QUANTITY BROUGHT TO MARKET

A supply schedule or supply curve

68

This corresponds with common sense: Sellers will try to sell more when the price is high, and buyers will try to buy more when the price is low.

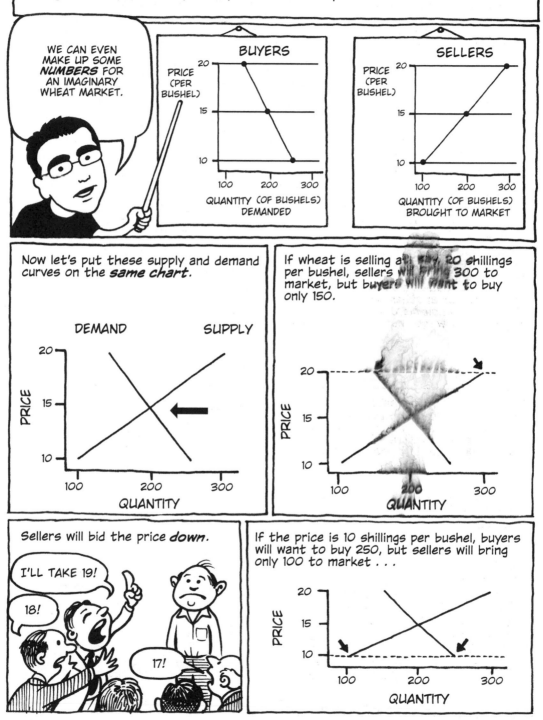

WE CAN EVEN MAKE UP SOME **NUMBERS** FOR AN IMAGINARY WHEAT MARKET.

BUYERS

PRICE (PER BUSHEL)

QUANTITY (OF BUSHELS) DEMANDED

SELLERS

PRICE (PER BUSHEL)

QUANTITY (OF BUSHELS) BROUGHT TO MARKET

Now let's put these supply and demand curves on the **same chart**.

DEMAND   SUPPLY

PRICE

QUANTITY

If wheat is selling at say, 20 shillings per bushel, sellers will bring 300 to market, but buyers will want to buy only 150.

PRICE

QUANTITY

Sellers will bid the price **down**.

I'LL TAKE 19!

18!

17!

If the price is 10 shillings per bushel, buyers will want to buy 250, but sellers will bring only 100 to market . . .

PRICE

QUANTITY

and buyers will bid the price **up**.

I'LL PAY 11!

12!

Price gravitates toward the intersection, the **equilibrium**. Once it's there, there's no reason for it to move; sellers bring exactly as much as buyers want to buy. It's only a small jump to say:

200 BUSHELS WILL BE SOLD AT 15 SHILLINGS APIECE!

We can visualize changes in supply and demand by **moving** the lines. If supply goes up, like in a good harvest, the market finds a new equilibrium where more is sold at a lower price.

That's just a taste; there are all sorts of subtle, sophisticated ways to manipulate the chart. The supply-demand model of price became the new foundation of economic models as soon as it appeared in Alfred Marshall's *Principles of Economics* in 1890.

On page 40, we saw Marshall warning against taking Ricardo's models too seriously. To his credit, Marshall said the same about his **own** model.

"ITS LIMITATIONS ARE SO CONSTANTLY OVERLOOKED, ESPECIALLY BY THOSE WHO APPROACH IT FROM AN ABSTRACT POINT OF VIEW, THAT THERE IS A DANGER IN THROWING IT INTO *DEFINITE FORM AT ALL.*"

He even called his subject **economics** instead of **political economy**; he thought the subject was too **abstract** to be a guide to policy.

SOMEDAY WE'LL *"RETURN TO REALITY,"* THOUGH.

PRINCIPLES OF ECONOMICS

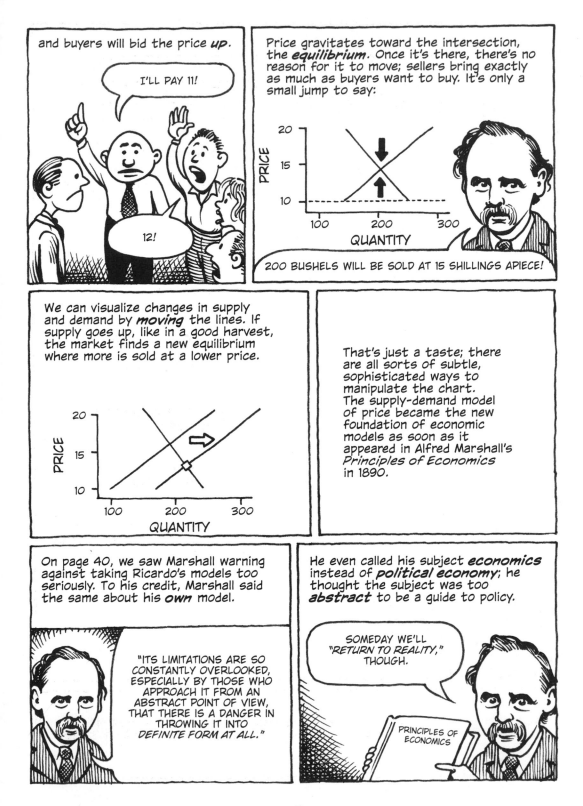

THIS NEW ECONOMICS WAS ALSO CALLED **NEOCLASSICAL** ECONOMICS, BECAUSE IT KEPT RICARDO'S CLASSICAL METHODS — IT WAS STILL A SYSTEM OF LOGICAL MODELS, BASED ON SIMPLIFYING ASSUMPTIONS THAT MAY NOT HOLD TRUE IN THE REAL WORLD. HERE ARE A FEW OF THOSE ASSUMPTIONS:

- *Economic man* (page 37) rationally pursues his own self-interest

- Supply and demand stay put unless you move them, which means

  - o Incomes stay the same

  - o Tastes stay the same

  - o Other prices stay the same

- Everyone has the same information

- All buyers and sellers are so small that their actions can't affect a good's price

But even as these new models were being invented, the real world was making a *hash* of that last assumption, notably in America, so let's head back there.

The public be damned.

　　　　—William H. Vanderbilt (1882)

CHAPTER 3

THE
MONEY
POWER

(1865–1914)

After the Civil War, the slaves were free, the West was open ...

CHEAP LAND AND HIGH WAGES FOREVER!

but the South didn't change as much as expected. The rich may not have owned slaves anymore, but they still owned the land.

ALMOST AS GOOD!

And the North had a *new* problem: Businesses had grown big and powerful during the war, and they weren't about to stop.

AMERICA GETS RAILROADED

ONE REASON BUSINESSES GOT BIG: THEY TOOK ON BIG *PROJECTS*.

Like the *transcontinental railroad*. It was clearly needed, but who would cover the huge costs?

IF WE WAIT FOR A PRIVATE RAILROAD TO REACH CALIFORNIA, WE'LL WAIT FOREVER.

Washington had the resources—the federal government *owned* most of the West—but Americans were *wary* of government power.

It seemed safer to encourage *private* entrepreneurs.

YOU WIN *FREE LAND* ON BOTH SIDES OF THE TRACKS! PLUS LOANS AND GRANTS FOR THE *ENTIRE COST*!

UNION PACIFIC

CENTRAL PACIFIC

The transcontinental railroad was completed in 1869, but nobody made sure the money was well spent.

WHY DOES IT GO LIKE THIS?

THE GOVERNMENT PAYS PER MILE!

The federal government wound up handing railroad companies—or almost anyone who claimed to be a railroad—enough land to fill most of *Texas*; states gave them *more*.

And if people expected public spirit in return, well . . .

HOW MUCH?

TICKETS

HOW MUCH YOU GOT?

Railroads could charge ludicrous amounts because they were *natural monopolies*—one railway from point A to point B may make sense, but not two parallel lines. So the *first* railroad is the *only* railroad.

TAKE IT OR LEAVE IT.

BUT WE *GAVE* YOU THE LAND AND MONEY TO BUILD YOUR LINE IN THE FIRST PLACE!

STILL, RAILROADS TIED THE ECONOMY TOGETHER. THEY MADE THE U.S. INTO ONE BIG MARKET, WHICH MEANT HUGE *ECONOMIES OF SCALE* FOR COMPANIES BIG ENOUGH TO TAKE ADVANTAGE.

Economies of scale apply when making things in bigger batches is cheaper. They usually involve a trade-off: lower *per-unit* cost, but higher *up-front* cost.

A BIG FACTORY CAN MAKE STEEL AT A LOW COST PER TON, BUT FIRST YOU HAVE TO BUILD THE FACTORY!

The first person to pay that up-front cost has a huge advantage, and is well set up to grow even *bigger*.

Eventually that high setup cost keeps competitors out as effectively as any law.

BLACKSMITH SHOP

I'D LIKE TO COMPETE. IF ONLY I COULD AFFORD TO BUILD A FACTORY AS BIG AS A CITY.

Economies of scale operated with a vengeance in the late 19th century. Big businesses got bigger, while their founders grew unimaginably rich.

NEW YORK

CALIFORNIA

CHICAGO

Philip Armour (1832-1901) Meat

Cornelius Vanderbilt (1794-1877) Railroads

Cyrus McCormick (1809-1884) Farm machines

PITTSBURGH

Andrew Carnegie (1835-1919) Steel

Andrew Mellon (1855-1937) Carnegie's banker

Leland Stanford (1824-1893) Railroads

Richard Sears (1863-1914) Mail-order goods

Washington Duke (1820-1905) Tobacco

NORTH CAROLINA

How big was big? There was *no limit*; a single company could engulf an entire industry. Consider:

BIG OIL (AND OTHER BIG THINGS)

The oil business got its start when someone refined crude oil into cheap *kerosene*, which worked in lamps.

The first oil well was drilled in Pennsylvania in 1859; soon small drillers and refiners competed in free-market fashion.

FOUR CENTS A CAN!

THREE!

TWO FOR FIVE CENTS!

KEROSENE KEROSENE KEROSENE KEROSENE

Then came the Panic of 1873, the worst crash yet, set off by a chain of bank failures all over the world.

Big firms survive crashes better than small ones. By 1880, John D. Rockefeller's Standard Oil had bought some competitors, allied with others, and smashed the rest.

SCHEISSE!

MERDE!

GOSH!

A MONOPOLY!

STANDARD OIL   STANDARD OIL   STANDARD OIL   STANDARD OIL

6¢ A CAN   6¢ A CAN   6¢ A CAN   6¢ A CAN

Technically, *monopoly* only applies to sellers; a buyer that has no competition is a *monopsony*. Standard Oil was monopoly *and* monopsony.

HE GETS YOU COMING AND GOING!

77

Standard Oil was never a total monopoly; it always had a few competitors here and there. But big companies could take control *without* being monopolies.

They could *buy up* . . .

suppliers

shippers

retailers

STANDARD OIL

STANDARD OIL REFINERY

STANDARD OIL

and *bully* the ones they didn't buy. (Standard Oil even bullied *railroads*.)

GIVE US A DOLLAR BACK FOR EVERY BARREL OF OIL WE SHIP.

OK . . .

AND A DOLLAR BACK FOR EVERY BARREL OUR *COMPETITORS* SHIP.

THAT'S INSANE!

DO IT OR WE'LL BUILD OUR OWN RAILROAD.

They could even *control* their competitors.

WHY DON'T YOU CUT YOUR PRICE AND TAKE HIS CUSTOMERS?

STANDARD OIL

INOFFENSIVE OIL

6¢ A CAN

6¢ A CAN

HE'D *CRUSH* ME IF I TRIED. HE TOLERATES ME AS LONG AS I STICK TO *HIS* PRICE.

These advantages of *bigness* existed in Adam Smith's day, too. But back then, the *disadvantages* outweighed them.

THIS SAYS THAT THE EDINBURGH OFFICE HAS ONLY ENOUGH MONEY TO LAST TWO DAYS.

PUT A CHEST OF SILVER ON A HORSE AND SEND IT TO THEM.

WHY BOTHER? THIS LETTER'S A WEEK OLD.

So a business that grew too big in the 18th century would collapse under its own weight unless government propped it up. This, as we saw on page 31, is why Adam Smith said:

LAISSEZ-FAIRE!

But a century later, *technology* had changed.

THE NEW YORK OFFICE NEEDS MONEY!

WIRE IT TO THEM!

THE ORE SHIPMENT WAS DELAYED!

TELEGRAPH MICHIGAN FOR MORE!

ONE OF THE DIRECTORS CAN'T MAKE THE MEETING!

INCLUDE HIM BY TELEPHONE!

Since then, the advantages of bigness have outweighed the disadvantages, and companies have been led, "as if by an invisible hand," to *get big* and *take over*.

THAT'S WHAT PAYS!

Getting big got easier in 1890, when New Jersey let corporations own *stock in other corporations*. That meant that one corporation could acquire another just by buying up its stock.

THE "BOSS OF THE UNITED STATES"

Enter J. P. Morgan (1837-1913), a big banker on New York's Wall Street. Wall Street was where the stocks of giant companies were traded, not always honestly.

Morgan preferred *order*; he **merged** the big players in industry after industry into super-corporations, or *trusts*.

And when J. P. Morgan organized a trust, he kept **control**. So a small group of businessmen—Morgan, Rockefeller, the railroad lords, and some others—**ran** a big chunk of the economy.

By the end of the 19th century, the United States had a *mixed economy*, with small businesses and farms side by side with a sort of *socialism*, run by big businesses.

George Perkins, a partner in Morgan's bank

Such order and planning was *needed*, because of the tension between rising initial costs and falling per-unit costs we saw on page 76.

"WHAT A BLESSING IT WAS THAT THE IDEA OF COOPERATION, WITH RAILROADS, WITH TELEGRAPH LINES, WITH STEEL COMPANIES, WITH OIL COMPANIES, CAME IN AND PREVAILED, TO TAKE THE PLACE OF THE CHAOTIC [FREE-MARKET] CONDITIONS...." —ROCKEFELLER

"WHAT'S THE DIFFERENCE BETWEEN THE U.S. STEEL CORPORATION, AS IT WAS ORGANIZED BY MR. MORGAN, AND A DEPARTMENT OF STEEL AS IT MIGHT BE ORGANIZED BY THE GOVERNMENT?"

That is, once you'd invested in one of those giant steel plants, you needed to sell *lots* of cheap steel to pay for it. You couldn't rely on the free market to supply your raw materials and ship the finished product—any interruption would *cost you money*.

By taking *control* of their suppliers, shippers, and so on, big business ensured *smooth production*. In the late 19th century, the steel mills of Pittsburgh ran 24-7.

So the economy was *managed*—but not for the benefit of the public.

"I OWE THE PUBLIC NOTHING."

Running the economy can be very profitable. The railroad tycoon Cornelius Vanderbilt died in 1877 with $100 million; John D. Rockefeller became the world's first **billionaire**. (By comparison, in 1888 the state of Massachusetts took in only $7 million in taxes.)

One　　A thousand　　A million　　　　A billion

THAT SORT OF MONEY CAN'T BE **EARNED** IN ANY REAL SENSE. IF YOU WORK HARD, SAVE YOUR PENNIES, AND PUT $100,000 IN YOUR MATTRESS EVERY YEAR, YOU'LL HAVE A BILLION DOLLARS A LITTLE AFTER 12,000 AD.

AND A VERY BIG MATTRESS!

It's also too much to **spend**. The heirs to these sums—even the morons and the drunks—stayed rich, simply because it's impossible to blow through a fortune that big.

And **political** power goes hand in hand with **economic** power. The government helped the rich with tariffs that kept competing goods out; immigration policies that let more workers in; a land policy that let mining, logging, and ranching businesses use public land for almost nothing (still the case today); and a foreign policy that pushed American interests abroad.

WHAT ARE OUR "INTERESTS"?

OUR BUSINESSES!

DOWN ON THE FARM

The Homestead Act (1862) had opened the West to settlement, and farmers had rushed in. Their lives should have been great; technology was finally reaching the farm.

FERTILIZER TO GROW MORE!

MACHINES TO HARVEST MORE!

RAILROADS TO HAUL IT AWAY!

AND BANKS TO FINANCE IT ALL!

BANK

But so many farmers settled so fast that soon there was **too much food.**

WHAT? IS THAT A TYPO?

SEE, DEMAND FOR FOOD IS RELATIVELY *INELASTIC*: IT DOESN'T CHANGE MUCH WHEN PRICE CHANGES. WE CAN'T DO WITHOUT IT WHEN IT'S EXPENSIVE, AND WE CAN'T EAT A TON WHEN IT'S CHEAP.

We can visualize *inelastic demand* as a nearly vertical demand curve.

DEMAND   SUPPLY

PRICE

QUANTITY

(The slope really depends on the scale you use, but it's still useful to think of it this way.)

When all these farms increased the supply of food, the price went way down.

DEMAND

SUPPLY

NEW PRICE

NEW QUANTITY

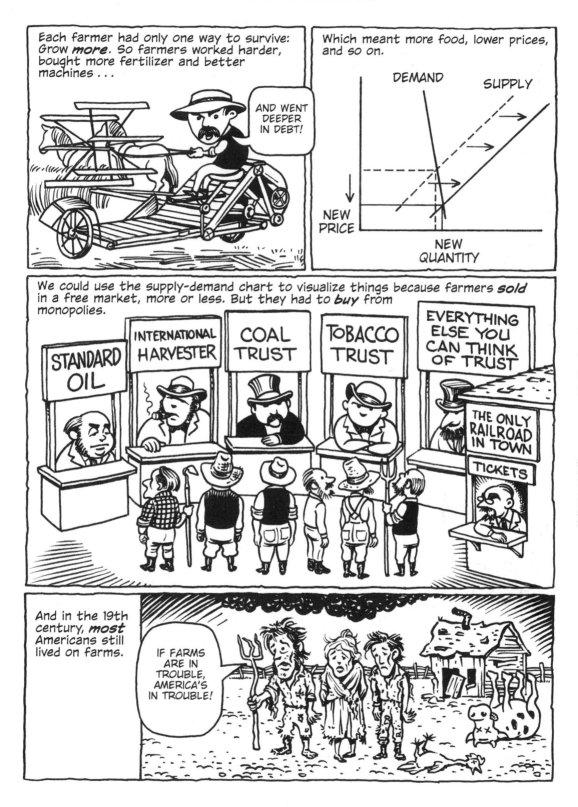

Each farmer had only one way to survive: Grow **more**. So farmers worked harder, bought more fertilizer and better machines ...

AND WENT DEEPER IN DEBT!

Which meant more food, lower prices, and so on.

DEMAND

SUPPLY

NEW PRICE

NEW QUANTITY

We could use the supply-demand chart to visualize things because farmers **sold** in a free market, more or less. But they had to **buy** from monopolies.

STANDARD OIL

INTERNATIONAL HARVESTER

COAL TRUST

TOBACCO TRUST

EVERYTHING ELSE YOU CAN THINK OF TRUST

THE ONLY RAILROAD IN TOWN

TICKETS

And in the 19th century, **most** Americans still lived on farms.

IF FARMS ARE IN TROUBLE, AMERICA'S IN TROUBLE!

TROUBLE AT WORK

With farms suffering and good land pretty much claimed, industrial workers lost their big bargaining chip.

GIMME A RAISE OR I'LL GRAB A FARM!

NO, YOU WON'T.

Their bargaining position got worse as new job hunters arrived by the steamship load.

THEY WORK CHEAP, CAN'T TALK TO ONE ANOTHER, AND CAN'T VOTE!

Big businesses controlled their *labor* supply like they controlled their other supplies. On page 81, we saw the steel mills of Pittsburgh running 24-7. Thing was, there were only *two shifts*—workers worked 12-hour days, 7 days a week.

Workers tried *immigrant bashing*.

More sensibly, they fought for *unions*. It was a real fight; bosses broke strikes with *private armies* . . .

"I can hire one half the working class to kill the other half." —Jay Gould (1836–1892), railroad tycoon

and when that failed, the *real* army.

Farms in trouble, workers in trouble—people started to realize that America had a problem.

SEE? SEE?

YIPE!

WALL STREET vs. MAIN STREET

What to do? People tried working through state legal systems, but in 1886, the Supreme Court *nullified* state controls with a wild and crazy interpretation of the Constitution.

A CORPORATION IS A *LEGAL PERSON*, AND AS A "PERSON," IT HAS A *CONSTI-TUTIONAL RIGHT* TO MAKE MONEY. STATES CAN'T INTERFERE!

RRRIP

Still doctrine today.

That left:

GET THEM!

WHO, ME?

In 1887, Congress, which can regulate interstate commerce, created the Interstate Commerce Commission to bring railroads to heel. It didn't work.

TAKE THAT!

In 1890, Congress tried really hard, with the Sherman Anti-Trust Act.

HA HA HA HA HA HA

"CONSPIRACIES IN RESTRAINT OF TRADE" ARE *ILLEGAL!*

But the law wasn't used— except against unions.

A UNION IS A "CONSPIRACY IN RESTRAINT OF TRADE"!

WHAT PART OF *"ANTI-TRUST ACT"* DON'T YOU UNDERSTAND?

JAIL

Part of the problem: The president enforces the law, but in the late 19th century the presidency was *weak*; presidents didn't do much more than *fume*.

"THIS IS A GOVERNMENT OF THE PEOPLE, BY THE PEOPLE, AND FOR THE PEOPLE NO LONGER. IT IS A GOVERNMENT OF CORPORATIONS, BY CORPORATIONS, AND FOR CORPORATIONS."

Rutherford Hayes, Republican, president from 1877–1881.

"[CORPORATIONS ARE] FAST BECOMING THE PEOPLE'S MASTERS...COMMUNISM IS A HATEFUL THING AND A MENACE TO PEACE AND ORGANIZED GOVERNMENT. BUT THE COMMUNISM OF COMBINED WEALTH AND CAPITAL, THE OUTGROWTH OF OVERWEENING CUPIDITY AND SELFISHNESS, WHICH INSIDIOUSLY UNDERMINES THE JUSTICE AND INTEGRITY OF FREE INSTITUTIONS, IS NOT LESS DANGEROUS THAN THE COMMUNISM OF OPPRESSED POVERTY AND TOIL."

Grover Cleveland, Democrat, president from 1885–1889 and 1893–1897.

That changed in 1901, when one Theodore Roosevelt, a Republican, took office.

THE PROGRESSIVES

President Teddy Roosevelt's program:

I'M FOR THE *SQUARE DEAL.*

SOUNDS HARMLESS.

But TR knew regular folks couldn't *get* a square deal with the rich controlling everything, hence the other part of his program: the *big stick.* TR broke up some trusts, protected public land from businesses, and controlled railroad rates.

TAKE THAT, *"MALEFACTORS OF GREAT WEALTH!"*

It turned out that for all of industrialists' rugged talk, it was easy to push them around.

ALL WE NEED IS THE POLITICAL WILL TO DO IT!

TR was the right person, but his presidency (1901-1909) was also the right time. People were riled up, partly thanks to investigative journalists, called *muckrakers.*

EEW.

For instance, TR's friend, the photojournalist Jacob Riis (1849-1914), investigated New York's slums and found that slumlords were often quite rich and could easily afford to maintain their buildings properly. In fact, slumdwellers paid *high rents*, enough to entitle them to decent housing.

TRUE IN MY TIME, TRUE A HUNDRED YEARS LATER!

Slums could be dealt with locally, with building codes and the like; so could working conditions, which were terrible.

In 1911, the Triangle Shirtwaist Factory fire in New York City killed 146 workers, mostly women and girls, who had been *locked in the factory*. The tragedy led to reforms all over the country.

But some problems weren't local. A Virginian might die from tainted beef that was raised in Kansas and canned in Illinois by a corporation chartered in Delaware and run from an office in New York by people who lived in Connecticut.

So when *The Jungle*, a 1906 novel by the muckraker Upton Sinclair, detailed how the giant meatpacking firms really operated...

PURE BEEF

President Teddy Roosevelt responded with the Pure Food and Drug Act (1906).

FEWER RATS IN THE BEEF!

TR was a new type of *liberal*. Liberals value individual *liberty*, which had always meant keeping government *weak*. Twentieth-century liberals gave government more *power*.

WE NEED *PUBLIC* POWER TO COUNTERBALANCE *PRIVATE* POWER!

TR's successor, William Howard Taft, became president in 1909. He kept the pressure on the trusts. The granddaddy of them all, Standard Oil, was broken up in 1911. We can get an idea how big it was by looking at its *pieces*.

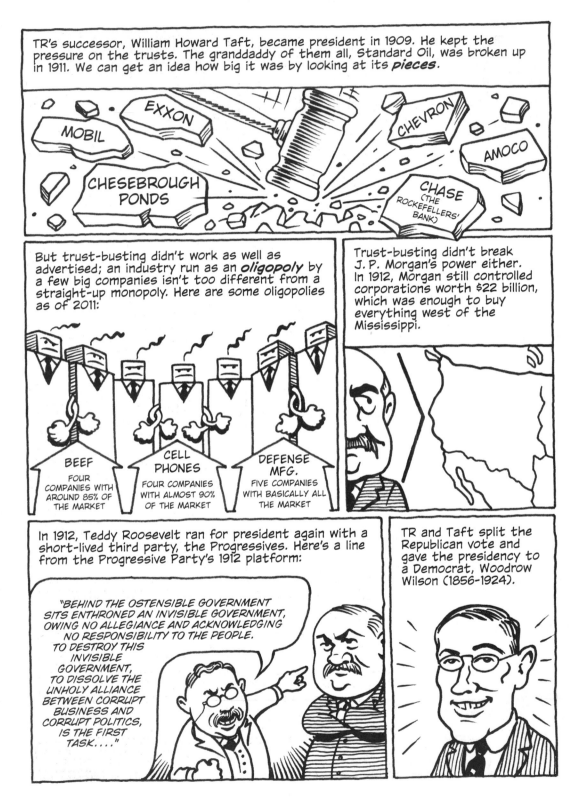

MOBIL

EXXON

CHEVRON

AMOCO

CHESEBROUGH PONDS

CHASE (THE ROCKEFELLERS' BANK)

But trust-busting didn't work as well as advertised; an industry run as an *oligopoly* by a few big companies isn't too different from a straight-up monopoly. Here are some oligopolies as of 2011:

BEEF
FOUR COMPANIES WITH AROUND 85% OF THE MARKET

CELL PHONES
FOUR COMPANIES WITH ALMOST 90% OF THE MARKET

DEFENSE MFG.
FIVE COMPANIES WITH BASICALLY ALL THE MARKET

Trust-busting didn't break J. P. Morgan's power either. In 1912, Morgan still controlled corporations worth $22 billion, which was enough to buy everything west of the Mississippi.

In 1912, Teddy Roosevelt ran for president again with a short-lived third party, the Progressives. Here's a line from the Progressive Party's 1912 platform:

"BEHIND THE OSTENSIBLE GOVERNMENT SITS ENTHRONED AN INVISIBLE GOVERNMENT, OWING NO ALLEGIANCE AND ACKNOWLEDGING NO RESPONSIBILITY TO THE PEOPLE. TO DESTROY THIS INVISIBLE GOVERNMENT, TO DISSOLVE THE UNHOLY ALLIANCE BETWEEN CORRUPT BUSINESS AND CORRUPT POLITICS, IS THE FIRST TASK...."

TR and Taft split the Republican vote and gave the presidency to a Democrat, Woodrow Wilson (1856-1924).

PRESIDENT WILSON DIDN'T HIT ANYONE WITH STICKS, BUT HE WAS A PROGRESSIVE, TOO. HIS ADMINISTRATION (1913-1921) IMPLEMENTED:

An *income tax* (1913), ranging from 1% on high incomes to 7% on very high incomes.

7%? AN OUTRAGE!

The *Clayton Antitrust Act* (1914), which can *prevent* monopolies and oligopolies from forming (easier than breaking them up later).

And the *Federal Reserve System* (1913), the first official central bank since the 1830s.

A central bank is an entity that regulates banks and controls the money supply. The Fed was, in part, designed to take these roles *away* from J. P. Morgan, who was the country's *unofficial* central bank.

President Cleveland asking Morgan for gold, 1895.

Morgan, by the way, died in 1913, leaving a *year's salary* to all his employees. He never helped himself to the billions he controlled; he died with $68 million. Or as Andrew Carnegie noted:

"And to think that he was not a rich man."

WHICH BRINGS US TO THE PROUD YEAR OF *1914.*

	Capital published	Panic of 1873	Panic of 1886	Panic of 1893 (very bad)	Pure Food and Drug Act	Wilson elected	
							Clayton Act
1865	1867	1869	1873	1879	1886	1890	1893	1901	1906	1907	1911	1912	1913	1914

Civil War ends

Standard Oil rules oil biz

Principles of Economics published

Standard Oil broken up

Transcontinental railroad completed

Morgan starts creating trusts

TR takes office

Panic of 1907

Federal Reserve and Income tax

THE GLOBAL ECONOMY

By 1914, the Industrial Revolution had transformed the Western world.

REMEMBER WHEN A TELEGRAPH WAS A BIG DEAL?

Western empires spread across the globe, grabbing resources and markets.

WHAT'S THAT?

Japan escaped Western control, perhaps because it has few natural resources worth stealing. Instead, Japan *industrialized*, importing raw materials and exporting finished goods, and carved out its own empire.

THE ONLY RESOURCE WE HAVE IS OUR *PEOPLE*.

The British Empire dominated the world. Here's the English economist William Stanley Jevons speaking in the late 19th century:

"THE PLAINS OF NORTH AMERICA AND RUSSIA ARE OUR CORNFIELDS; CHICAGO AND ODESSA OUR GRANARIES; CANADA AND THE BALTIC ARE OUR TIMBER FOREST; AUSTRALASIA CONTAINS OUR SHEEP FARMS, AND IN ARGENTINA AND ON THE WESTERN PRAIRIES OF NORTH AMERICA ARE OUR HERDS OF OXEN; PERU SENDS HER SILVER; AND THE GOLD OF SOUTH AFRICA AND AUSTRALIA FLOWS TO LONDON; THE HINDUS AND THE CHINESE GROW TEA FOR US, AND OUR COFFEE, SUGAR, AND SPICE PLANTATIONS ARE ALL IN THE INDIES. SPAIN AND FRANCE ARE OUR VINEYARDS AND THE MEDITERRANEAN OUR FRUIT GARDEN. . . ."

A British-dominated world was fine if you were British. But Germany's **mixed economy** had eclipsed Britain's more laissez-faire one, and Germans didn't see why Britain should stay on top.

IRON AND STEEL PRODUCTION, 1870 AND 1913
MILLIONS OF TONS

30
15
0

6.9 BRITAIN
2.1 GERMANY
1870

16.9 BRITAIN
27.4 GERMANY
1913

IT'S NOT *FAIR!*

Kaiser Wilhelm II (1859–1941) of Germany

This tension, and others, led European countries to stockpile weapons, which upped tensions, so everyone bought more weapons, and so on: an **arms race.**

THEY HAVE MORE THAN YOU!

THEY HAVE MORE THAN *YOU!*

ARMS CO.

ARMS CO.

Still, many people believed war would never come.

WAR WOULD DISRUPT OUR INTERDEPENDENT GLOBAL ECONOMY, TO THE POINT THAT IT WOULD BE *AGAINST OUR OWN INTEREST!* WAR IS *IRRATIONAL,* SO IT'S *IMPOSSIBLE!*

THAT PREDICTION WOULD HAVE WORKED OUT IF PEOPLE WERE RATIONAL. INSTEAD, WORLD WAR I STARTED, FOR NO GOOD REASON, IN AUGUST 1914. THE LINEUP: *ALLIES* (BRITAIN, FRANCE, RUSSIA, AND LATER ITALY) VS. *CENTRAL POWERS* (GERMANY, AUSTRIA-HUNGARY, AND LATER TURKEY).

WANNA FIGHT?

WE DO HAVE ALL THESE WEAPONS.

We have involved ourselves in a colossal
muddle, having blundered in the control of
a delicate machine, the working of which
we do not understand.

—John Maynard Keynes (1930)

CHAPTER 4

THINGS FALL APART

(1914–1945)

Mass-produced modern weapons made World War I battlefields not merely dangerous; they were **unfit for human life.**

Soldiers stayed alive by staying **underground**, in trenches.

Attacking the enemy trench meant leaving yours.

ALSO KNOWN AS SUICIDE.

The generals, safe in country estates, far from the slumlike trenches, kept ordering attacks. **Millions** of dead piled up.

I DON'T THINK I **LIKE** THE TWENTIETH CENTURY.

The battlefields were stalemated; the outcome of WWI was decided **elsewhere**.

ECONOMIES AT WAR

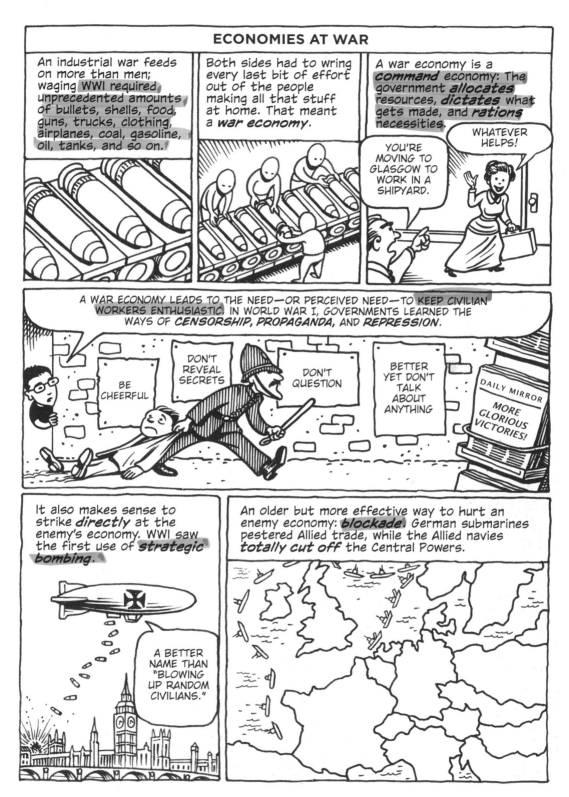

An industrial war feeds on more than men; waging WWI required unprecedented amounts of bullets, shells, food, guns, trucks, clothing, airplanes, coal, gasoline, oil, tanks, and so on.

Both sides had to wring every last bit of effort out of the people making all that stuff at home. That meant a *war economy*.

A war economy is a *command* economy: The government *allocates* resources, *dictates* what gets made, and *rations* necessities.

YOU'RE MOVING TO GLASGOW TO WORK IN A SHIPYARD.

WHATEVER HELPS!

A WAR ECONOMY LEADS TO THE NEED—OR PERCEIVED NEED—TO KEEP CIVILIAN WORKERS ENTHUSIASTIC. IN WORLD WAR I, GOVERNMENTS LEARNED THE WAYS OF *CENSORSHIP, PROPAGANDA,* AND *REPRESSION.*

BE CHEERFUL

DON'T REVEAL SECRETS

DON'T QUESTION

BETTER YET DON'T TALK ABOUT ANYTHING

DAILY MIRROR

MORE GLORIOUS VICTORIES!

It also makes sense to strike *directly* at the enemy's economy. WWI saw the first use of *strategic bombing.*

A BETTER NAME THAN "BLOWING UP RANDOM CIVILIANS."

An older but more effective way to hurt an enemy economy: *blockade.* German submarines pestered Allied trade, while the Allied navies *totally cut off* the Central Powers.

The U.S. was neutral, but with the Central Powers cut off, Americans traded only with the Allies, who paid *any* price for war materiel...

after borrowing the money from American banks.

And so:

WE *MUST* HELP THE ALLIES!

IF THEY LOSE, WHO'LL PAY US BACK?

J.P.Jr.

W.W.

Then in early 1917, the Russians overthrew their tsar, but stayed in the war.

LONG LIVE DEMOCRACY!

Now the Allies were all *democracies*, while the Central Powers were not. That was the sort of war President Wilson could support.

"THE WORLD MUST BE MADE SAFE FOR DEMOCRACY!"

WHATEVER!

J.P.Jr.

W.W.

Russia's democracy didn't last; in late 1917, Lenin, who we last saw on page 64, took over (and pulled out of WWI).

But it was too late for the Central Powers. Hungry and exhausted, they gave up in late 1918.

YOU WIN.

YAY.

WWI left a world of problems; the punitive Treaty of Versailles (1919) made things worse.

YOU GERMANS HAVE TO PAY US THE *FULL COST* OF THE WAR.

YOU'RE KIDDING.

NO.

In *The Economic Consequences of the Peace* (1919), John Maynard Keynes (1883-1946), a young British economist, tried to explain that Germany could earn the money only by *exporting goods*, while the Allies were also crippling German exports.

HOW WILL THEY PAY?

THAT'S *THEIR* PROBLEM.

The Allies never got most of the money, but not for lack of trying. They came up with plan after plan to keep Germany paying. Under one plan, Germany would have been paying until 1988.

DAWES PLAN

YOUNG PLAN

PLAN PLAN

France and Britain couldn't forgive Germany's debt because the U.S. wouldn't forgive theirs.

Germany tried to deal by *printing* extra money, then more, then more. All that money caused *inflation* (called that because when money loses its value, *prices* inflate).

At some point people lost faith in money, and without faith, money is nothing.

BREAD 20ℳ 50ℳ

10,00•
1 MILLION
1 BILLION •
200 BILLION

Cash wasn't worth saving, or even *stealing*.

10,00•
1 MILLION
1 BILLION •
200 BILLION
0ℳ

GERMANY FINALLY STOPPED THE INSANITY IN LATE 1923 BY *ABANDONING* ITS CURRENCY, PRINTING A NEW ONE, AND *NOT* PRINTING TOO MUCH OF IT.

BIG PLANS

Another consequence of WWI: People saw the incredible **power** of the industrial economy when it's **directed**.

REMEMBER WHAT WE ACHIEVED WHEN WE ALL FOLLOWED A *PLAN*?

MOUNTAINS OF DEAD?

WELL, YEAH, BUT WHAT IF THAT EFFORT WENT TO SOMETHING *GOOD*, LIKE HOSPITALS OR SCHOOLS?

But in a democracy, it's hard to keep people cooperating when there's no war.

YOU'RE MOVING TO ROME TO WORK IN AN ORPHANAGE.

BITE ME.

Benito Mussolini, an ex-socialist who took over Italy in 1922, had a solution: Get rid of democracy.

"ALL WITHIN THE STATE, NOTHING OUTSIDE THE STATE, NOTHING AGAINST THE STATE!"

Mussolini called his solution, which was a sort of permanent war economy, *Fascism*.

One supreme leader

In bed with big business

Wartime-style repression

Propaganda and censorship

Some benefits to keep people happy

HOSPITAL

Easy wars against weak countries

SOLINI GREAT

DAILY TIMES

MUSSOLINI IS GREAT

Today we see Mussolini as a bozo, but back then he seemed modern and dynamic. Dictators took over country after country in the 1920s. And not just capitalist countries.

REDS: The Russian Revolution and the Soviet State

Back to Russia: Lenin took over back on page 98. But what was supposed to happen **after** the revolution?

Capital

IT'S NOT IN HERE!

Engels had said the **state would wither away** under communism, but Lenin liked power, and anyway he couldn't relax while half of Russia, helped by the rest of the world, was trying to get rid of him (the **Russian Civil War**).

So Russian-style "communism" came to mean a **war economy**, complete with squashed dissent . . .

Brits and Americans

Other Russians

and government control of everything.

IN THE NAME OF THE PEOPLE! DON'T YOU KNOW THERE'S A WAR ON?

Czechs (!)

Poles

By the time the communists won, their prize was a hungry, angry country.

Other Russians

EVERY MONTH WE GET LESS. IT'S ALMOST LIKE PEOPLE WON'T **MAKE** STUFF IF THEY KNOW WE'RE GOING TO **TAKE** IT!

HOW ODD.

In 1921 Lenin did something unusual for a revolutionary: he **backpedaled**, letting small businesses run without too much interference, and letting farmers keep what they grew and sell it.

SO WE'RE GIVING UP POWER?

OF COURSE NOT. WE STILL RUN RAILROADS, HEAVY INDUSTRY, BANKING, MINING — THE **"COMMANDING HEIGHTS"** OF THE ECONOMY.

Lenin's "New Economic Policy" was a mixed economy, and mixed economies work. The Union of Soviet Socialist Republics (the country's new name) got on its feet.

BREAD
·CHEAP·

Then in 1924, Lenin died.

BEWARE OF STAL—*urk!*

WHAT DID HE SAY?

NOTHING.

Several top communists wanted to succeed Lenin; *Joseph Stalin* (1878-1953), a top party official, won.

We'll get back to Stalin later; for now, we'll just note that the mere survival of a communist state *inspired* people all over the world...

and *scared the bejesus* out of other people all over the world.

THE REVENGE OF WALL STREET

In the U.S., a post-WWI *red scare* helped establish a new conservative mood and give the 1920 presidential election to Warren Harding. Harding was a Republican, but he was no Teddy Roosevelt.

"I AM NOT FIT FOR THIS OFFICE AND NEVER SHOULD HAVE BEEN HERE."

True!

TREASURY

Harding died in office in 1923. His vice president and successor, Calvin Coolidge, was no more fit for the presidency than Harding had been, but he didn't say so.

In fact, "Silent Cal" barely said, or did, anything. The banker Andrew Mellon (page 76), now secretary of the Treasury, ran things. "Three presidents served under Mellon," people used to say.

ZZZZZ

Mellon's program: transferring the contents of the Treasury to himself and his friends.

HERE'S A TAX CUT!

AND ANOTHER!

AND REBATES OF TAXES YOU ALREADY PAID!

President Coolidge didn't even try to stop the corruption, but his idleness looked like wisdom as a *boom* got rolling.

THE ROARING TWENTIES

One reason for the boom: Many *technologies* were coming into their own.

IT'S A NEW ERA!

THIS BOOM WILL NEVER END!

For instance, *cars* had been around for decades, but they were luxuries. Then came *Henry Ford* (1863-1947), a strange man with strange ideas, like:

CARS FOR ALL!

In 1908, Ford built the reliable Model T, cheap at $850 or so. Orders poured in; to keep up, the factory became more and more efficient until it had an *assembly line*.

Assembly-line work is pretty wretched; at one point half of Ford's workers quit every month. Then Ford had another strange idea:

PAY WORKERS WELL!

In 1914, Ford started paying *five dollars* for an *eight-hour* day.

An "economic crime"! —*The Wall Street Journal*

Back then a steelworker made *one* dollar for *twelve* hours.

ISN'T *THAT* AN ECONOMIC CRIME?

SUPPLY AND DEMAND!

Ford's five-dollar day wasn't just generosity or wackiness—it kept workers on the assembly line, which was so efficient that the cost *per car* fell. Instead of pocketing the difference, Ford *lowered the price*. The Model T eventually sold for less than $300.

LOWER PRICES → MORE SALES → ECONOMIES OF SCALE

Ford's strange ideas could be bad, like making the *exact same 1908* car year after year. You couldn't even choose the color.

"ANY CUSTOMER CAN HAVE A CAR PAINTED ANY COLOR THAT HE WANTS AS LONG AS IT IS BLACK."

Some of Ford's rivals merged into General Motors (GM). They kept their separate car models, which gave buyers a *choice,* from the Chevrolet to the exalted Cadillac.

CHEVROLET

CADILLAC

And GM improved its cars, making Ford's Model T (and later Model A) obsolete. As Ford (the company) struggled, Ford (the man) wound up ruling his workers with *thugs* and spreading conspiracy theories.

INTERNATIONAL JEWS! HYPHENATED AMERICANS!

Still, by the end of the 1920s, *half* of U.S. households had cars, and Henry Ford deserves much of the credit.

WORKERS IN CARS?

WHAT'S NEXT? YACHTS?

BUSINESS RULES

Business leaders got all the credit for the boom. The public adored them like never before.

WALL ST.

This outpouring of love wasn't entirely spontaneous. Companies had mastered wartime-style *propaganda* (renamed "*public relations*," which sounds better).

DAILY BREAD

TRUST BUSINESS-MEN!

All the clapping drowned out some *inconvenient facts*:

The dead weight of the **WWI debts** pressed heavily on the world's economy.

IF YOU FORGIVE THE ALLIES' DEBT TO US, THEY'LL FORGIVE GERMANY'S DEBT. YOU COULD PREVENT ANOTHER WAR!

NO. "THEY HIRED THE MONEY, DIDN'T THEY?"

Farmers were barely getting by...

and wages **stagnated**, to the point that people didn't really own all their appliances and cars. Many had been bought with **consumer credit**, another 1920s innovation.

WANT A WASHING MACHINE?

WE CAN'T AFFORD IT.

SURE YOU CAN! YOU'RE PREAPPROVED!

So workers bought what they made, but with **borrowed money**.

MONEY THAT SHOULD HAVE BEEN OUR **WAGES** IN THE FIRST PLACE!

But all that was hidden, unlike the very public and very happy **Dow Jones index** of the stock market.

DOW JONES INDEX

Of course, the Dow isn't the economy; it's the average stock price of 30 big companies.

But in the 1920s, nobody reported **gross domestic product** (page 141) or other **broad** measures of the economy. The Dow Jones index was **the** economic number, and numbers are compelling.

THE ECONOMY IS BEAUTIFUL.

FAR OUT!

To understand what was happening, let's look at something called a **bubble**.

People buy something **because** the price is rising.

The buying drives up the price.

Almost any market can form a bubble. Bubbles happened in tulips in the Netherlands in the 17th century and Beanie Babies in the U.S. in the 20th century.

$10!

$15!

$40!

YOU WANT A CHEAP TOY THAT MUCH?

I DON'T WANT IT AT ALL. I WANT TO MAKE MONEY!

BUYING SOMETHING **ONLY** BECAUSE YOU EXPECT THE PRICE TO RISE SO YOU CAN RESELL IS CALLED **SPECULATION**.

BUBBLES ARE HARD TO VISUALIZE WITH THE SUPPLY-DEMAND CHART BECAUSE THERE'S NO *EQUILIBRIUM*: HIGHER PRICES INCREASE DEMAND, WHICH RAISES PRICES, AND SO ON.

Paying such inflated prices may seem foolish, but it can be *rational* to buy as long as you expect to find a *greater fool* to unload on before . . .

the bubble pops.

WHO'LL TAKE $35? I PAID $40 YESTERDAY!

$30!

$20!

$5!

$2.99!

By the late 1920s, stock prices were a bubble. J. P. Morgan might have stepped in to cool things down, but he was gone.

J. P. Morgan Jr., like many of his generation, inherited extraordinary *wealth* and *power* while being rather ordinary otherwise.

Republicans rode the euphoria to another victory in the presidential election of 1928; Coolidge woke up long enough to step aside for Herbert Hoover.

In late 1929, the stock market stumbled. Worse, many investors had bought stocks with **borrowed money**. So as stocks fell:

Lenders got nervous and demanded their money back...

to raise the money, some investors had to sell their stock...

so lenders got more nervous...

which drove prices down...

and so on.

At first people weren't worried.

I HEAR WALL STREET GOT REAMED!

SERVES 'EM RIGHT!

But nervous lenders weren't making new loans.

BANK

GO AWAY!

And many farms and businesses depend on loans; without new loans, they couldn't pay back their old loans.

OUR SAVINGS?

BANK

GONE.

OUT OF BUSINESS

And so began the **worst slump ever**.

THE GREAT DEPRESSION

In 1932, unemployment hit **25%**.

"WHEN MORE AND MORE PEOPLE ARE THROWN OUT OF WORK, UNEMPLOYMENT RESULTS."

Former President Coolidge, demonstrating why being *silent* worked so well for him.

Charity was exhausted, and anyway, proud workers often *killed* themselves rather than beg (*altruistic suicide*).

DIDN'T WANT TO BURDEN THE NEIGHBORS

With so little money around, prices *deflated* (the opposite of inflation, which we saw on page 99), but that happened to some products more than others. Farmers burned corn for heat because it wasn't worth selling...

WHILE COAL MINERS STARVE!

while industrialists often *cut output* rather than prices, because they couldn't cut their costs, especially wages.

MORE $

MORE WAGES

It may seem odd that it can be easier to *fire* people than to make them take a pay cut, but there you have it.

Whether workers got fired or took pay cuts, consumers had less money, because most consumers were workers.

GOING-OUT-OF-BUSINESS SALE

President Hoover made some money available, but Treasury Secretary Mellon gave the money only to *banks*, including his own bank. The banks *sat* on the money.

BANK

In November 1932, the voters replaced Hoover with a Democrat, Franklin Delano Roosevelt (1882-1945; Teddy's distant cousin).

I'M NOT HOOVER!

GOOD ENOUGH.

112

But FDR wouldn't take office until March of 1933. Meanwhile, the mood was getting ugly.

EMPLOYMENT O

J. P. MORGAN JR. HASN'T PAID A DIME IN TAXES IN YEARS!

MELLON HAD TREASURY EMPLOYEES FIND *TAX LOOPHOLES* FOR HIM ON *GOVERNMENT TIME!*

AND MELLON TELLS *US* TO BE MORAL?

Everything started to break down. Farmers and workers took over towns; the citizens of Dayton, Ohio, made plans to become a self-sufficient city-state.

I CALL I GET TO BE BARON!

I WANT TO BE BARON!

"If this country ever needed a Mussolini, it needs one now!"
—Senator David Reed of Pennsylvania.

"THE NATION IS ON THE VERGE OF CHAOS!"
—HOOVER

In one week hoarders yanked 15% of the money out of circulation....

By the time Herbert Hoover left office, more than a third of the banks in the country had failed.

BANK

GONE FISHING

113

THE HUNDRED DAYS

FDR delivered a *fighting speech* at his inauguration on March 4, 1933.

"THE RULERS OF THE EXCHANGE OF MANKIND'S GOODS HAVE FAILED, THROUGH THEIR OWN STUBBORNNESS AND THEIR OWN INCOMPETENCE.... THEY HAVE NO VISION, AND WHERE THERE IS NO VISION, THE PEOPLE PERISH. THE MONEY CHANGERS HAVE FLED FROM THEIR HIGH SEATS IN THE TEMPLE OF OUR CIVILIZATION. WE MAY NOW RESTORE THAT TEMPLE TO THE ANCIENT TRUTHS."

The key point:

"THE ONLY THING WE HAVE TO FEAR IS FEAR ITSELF."

In the first hundred days of his administration, FDR stopped the immediate emergency by fearlessly trying *everything*.

SHUT DOWN *ALL* BANKS!

NOW REOPEN THEM!

GET MONEY TO THE UNEMPLOYED!

GET WALL STREET UNDER CONTROL!

TAKE THE DOLLAR OFF THE GOLD STANDARD!

PRINT $2 BILLION BACKED BY BANK ASSETS!

WHAT DOES "BACKED BY BANK ASSETS" *MEAN*?

WHO CARES?

Then, by trial and error, a permanent program emerged.

THE NEW DEAL

After some false starts, FDR's program—the *New Deal*—came down to letting private business run more or less freely, but with *new institutions* to counteract the predictable *problems*.

One problem: Private business usually can't seem to provide work for everyone who wants it.

The *Works Progress Administration* (WPA), *Public Works Administration* (PWA), and *Civilian Conservation Corps* (CCC) provided jobs to the unemployed, while making useful things like bridges, tunnels, parks, and forests.

Failing that, *unemployment insurance* made sure people had income for a while after being laid off.

Private business also has no use for workers who can't work.

The *Social Security Administration* (SSA) provided old-age pensions and disability insurance.

The SSA also administered survivors' benefits and unemployment insurance, but when people talk about "Social Security" they usually mean the old-age pensions.

In a free market, the wild fluctuations of *farm prices* make it hard for farmers to do business.

The *Agricultural Adjustment Administration* (AAA) bought food in good harvests and sold it in bad ones, keeping food prices stable.

115

Another problem with private business: the point of *finance* is to turn paper savings into real investment.

UNDER CONSTRUCTION

But real investment pays back slowly, while *speculation* offers big profits right now. Speculation can *divert* money from real investment.

WALL ST.

WHY BOTHER MAKING 5% PROFIT A YEAR WHEN I CAN MAKE 10% IN A DAY?

CONSTRUCTION SUSPENDED

So the New Deal *regulated* finance.

For instance, the *Federal Deposit Insurance Corporation* (FDIC) insured banks so depositors could get their money back if a bank failed. In exchange, banks had to invest *soberly*.

And it wasn't just speculation—*outright fraud* was a big problem in the 1920s and 1930s. For instance, *commercial* banks—the type we saw on page 50—take deposits, invest the money, and keep the profit.

BANK

BANK

Panel 1:

Investment banks connect buyers with issuers of securities—stocks, bonds (IOUs that have to be paid back at a set time), and so on.

Panel 2:

In the 1930s, investment banks and commercial banks were often the *same bank*. During the Depression, banks could dump their own bad investments on their investment-banking clients.

PERU'S ABOUT TO DEFAULT. THE BONDS WE BOUGHT WILL BE WORTHLESS.

YOU KNOW WHAT YOU NEED? PERUVIAN BONDS!

Panel 3:

The Glass-Steagall Act (1933) *split* investment banks and commercial banks, neatly removing that temptation.

INVESTMENT BANK

REGULAR BANK

Panel 4:

AS FAR AS I'M CONCERNED, THAT'S A PERFECT EXAMPLE OF HOW REGULATION *SHOULD* BE DONE: NOT TANGLED REGULATIONS ENFORCED BY ARMIES OF INSPECTORS, BUT SIMPLE RULES THAT ALIGN *PRIVATE INCENTIVES* WITH THE *PUBLIC INTEREST*.

Panel 5:

There were lots of other regulations for Wall Street, presided over by the *Securities and Exchange Commission* (SEC). The first head of the SEC was Joseph Kennedy, one of the titans of finance in the 1920s.

BUT HE'S A SLEAZY WALL STREETER!

EXACTLY! HE KNOWS ALL THE TRICKS!

Panel 6:

The net result: Finance became *placid*. For the next forty-odd years, there were no big bubbles, no big crashes, and bankers lived by the "3-6-3" rule.

WE TAKE DEPOSITS AT 3%, LEND THE MONEY AT 6%, AND HIT THE GOLF COURSE AT 3 P.M.!

THE NEW DEAL CREATED AN ALPHABET SOUP OF PROGRAMS, ALL OF WHICH NEEDED *FUNDING*. AND ONE THING THE DEPRESSION DEPRESSED WAS *TAX REVENUES*. FDR *BORROWED* THE MONEY INSTEAD, FROM ANYONE WHO WOULD BUY A GOVERNMENT BOND.

NYA · SSA · WPA · AAA · CCC · NRA · TVA · SEC · CWA · FDIC · REA · WTF · CWP · OMG · PWA

This **deficit spending** drove orthodox economists bonkers.

YOU HAVE TO WAIT UNTIL TAX MONEY COMES IN BEFORE YOU SPEND IT!

IF WE DON'T SPEND MONEY NOW, THERE'LL BE NO MONEY OUT THERE FOR US TO TAX!

ECON 101

Economists went more bonkers when FDR put the dollar back on the gold standard in 1934, because he made it *illegal* to own gold except jewelry. So people could turn in paper dollars for gold, but then they couldn't own the gold.

WHAT DOES THAT EVEN MEAN?

Was that arrangement even a real gold standard? One thing it definitely was: an example of how FDR would try things that made no sense in standard economics.

IF IT WORKS IN PRACTICE, WHO CARES IF IT WORKS IN THEORY?

In one respect, FDR was strictly laissez-faire; he wouldn't let rich folks use the army, either to keep Latin Americans in line or to break *unions*.

I WANT TO PLAY WITH MY SOLDIERS!

LABOR PAINS

It might seem like the Depression should have been bad for unions, what with workers so desperate.

SWEATCO

But in fact the Depression *radicalized* many workers.

THE BOSSES DON'T KNOW WHAT THEY'RE DOING!

CLOSED

One radical tactic: the *sit-down strike*, where instead of standing outside the workplace and hoping other workers don't take their jobs...

PLEASE
PRETTY PLEASE
SUGAR ON TOP

the strikers *take over.*

ON
OFF

PLEASE
PRETTY PLEASE

Workers sat down in key General Motors plants in 1936; they fought off the police, and FDR wouldn't send the army.

HAVE YOU TRIED *NEGOTIATING*?

COMMIE!

GM gave in; the workers formed the giant United Auto Workers union (UAW). The UAW won good pay and hours, and that opened the floodgates. Other big industries were soon unionized, to the point that the *eight-hour day*—labor's goal since the 1870s—finally became the norm; a 1938 law mandating *overtime pay* made it official.

THE SECOND DEPRESSION

By 1936 the economy was humming again, and FDR easily won reelection.

"WE HAVE ALWAYS KNOWN THAT HEEDLESS SELF-INTEREST WAS BAD MORALS; WE KNOW NOW THAT IT IS BAD ECONOMICS."

"IN THE LONG RUN ECONOMIC MORALITY PAYS."

FDR never liked deficit spending, and now he cut back.

NO MORE GOVERNMENT JOBS?

PRIVATE BUSINESS WILL HIRE YOU! THINGS ARE GOING BACK TO NORMAL!

Business didn't pick up the slack; the result was a second depression, or a second dip in the main Depression.

SOUP

THIS IS NORMAL?

SEEMS TO BE.

BREAD

AS LATE AS 1939, UNEMPLOYMENT WAS OFFICIALLY 17%. THAT SOUNDED WORSE THAN IT WAS—PEOPLE WITH WPA AND CCC JOBS WERE COUNTED AS "UNEMPLOYED" FOR SOME REASON— BUT STILL, WHILE THE NEW DEAL EASED THE DEPRESSION, IT NEVER FIXED IT.

ON THE BRIGHT SIDE, SOMEONE HAD FIGURED OUT HOW TO FIX IT.

RETURN TO REALITY: Keynes and the General Theory

That someone was John Maynard Keynes, who we last saw on page 99. Keynes's key idea was simple: In slumps, spending falls, so to cure a slump:

SPEND MORE!

That was an old, common-sense idea. But most economists had ignored it.

ONLY A *SIMPLETON* WOULD SAY SOMETHING SO. . . SO. . .

SO *OBVIOUS.*

WE ALREADY KNOW WHAT TO DO ABOUT SLUMPS. *NOTHING!*

WAIT FOR THE ECONOMY TO CORRECT ITSELF!

APPLES 5¢

HERE'S THE *PROOF.* WHEN SPENDING FALLS, THE MONEY THAT ISN'T SPENT IS SAVED, SO THE SUPPLY OF LOANABLE FUNDS RISES.

WITH MORE SUPPLY, THE *PRICE* OF LOANS— THE INTEREST RATE—FALLS.

DEMAND SUPPLY

INTEREST RATE (THE *PRICE OF LOANS*)

LESS AMOUNT BORROWED MORE

LOW INTEREST LEADS TO MORE INVESTMENT: IF YOU HAVE AN INVESTMENT THAT WILL PAY 5% A YEAR, YOU *WON'T* BORROW MONEY FOR IT AT 7% INTEREST, AND YOU *WILL* AT 3%. SO LESS SPENDING MEANS MORE SAVING, WHICH MEANS MORE INVESTMENT, WHICH IS JUST ANOTHER FORM OF SPENDING. AND SO SPENDING GOES BACK UP AND THE SLUMP ENDS!

That logic convinced many people and baffled most of the rest.

BUT THE DEPRESSION'S *NOT* ENDING....

SURE IT IS! ANY DAY NOW!

121

Keynes said government could **counter** the business cycle by doing the **opposite** of everyone else.

THE GOVERNMENT SHOULD ACT CRAZY!

In a slump, Keynes said to pump up the economy with **deficit spending**.

In a boom, tax **more** and spend **less**, refilling the treasury and deflating 1920s-style lunacy.

THIS THINKING WAS NEW TO MOST ECONOMISTS, BUT FDR WAS ALREADY DEFICIT SPENDING.

BECAUSE I **IGNORE** ECONOMISTS!

THEN WHY WON'T THE DEPRESSION **END**?

COME ON, ALREADY!

Keynes's answer: FDR hadn't spent enough. Keynes recommended a **full-employment deficit**, a level of spending that would result in a deficit even if everyone had a job and paid taxes. Even **wasteful** spending would be better than nothing, because the workers and suppliers would **re-spend** the money they earned on useful things.

BUILD **PYRAMIDS** IF YOU HAVE TO!

Little did anyone know a big spending project was on the way: World War II.

YAY?

THE WORLD UNHINGED

World War II had many causes; the worldwide Depression was a big one. Hard times don't just change interest rates and employment numbers; they *drive people nuts*.

In the 1930s, collapsing trade hit *Japan*, which traded for almost everything, especially hard. The Japanese government fell apart; the army, out of control, attacked China to get resources.

But looting cost more and brought in less than just buying. And the Japanese army's brutality provoked *international embargoes*.

NOW WE NEED EVEN MORE RESOURCES.

MAYBE WE SHOULD ATTACK SOMEONE ELSE?

Plus, Japan never fully conquered China. The Chinese leader, Chiang Kai-shek (1887-1975), held out, and some Chinese *communists* survived, led by one Mao Zedong (1893-1976).

CHINA

The Chinese communists were stuck in the hills, far from the workers in the cities.

MAKES IT HARD TO HAVE A WORKERS' REVOLUTION.

With nothing else to do, the communists organized nearby *farmers*. The only capital that mattered in the Chinese countryside was *land*, so sharing capital meant dividing the land, also known as *land reform*. That was simple and practical once the landlord's objections were overcome.

YOU WORK THE SAME FIELD YOU ALWAYS HAVE, BUT NOW YOU KEEP WHAT YOU GROW INSTEAD OF GIVING IT TO THE LANDLORD.

MAY HE REST IN PEACE.

Maoist land reform didn't resemble anything imagined by Karl Marx. Neither did what was going on in the USSR....

We last saw the U.S.S.R. as Joseph Stalin consolidated power in the late 1920s. At the time, Soviets needed industrial goods, but the industrialized West wouldn't *trade* with commies, at least not openly.

The U.S. didn't even recognize the U.S.S.R. until 1933.

If you can't trade for something, you might as well make it.

WE'LL INDUSTRIALIZE!

5 YEAR PLAN

Stalin's plans undid Lenin's New Economic Policy (page 102). The state took charge of the whole economy. In the countryside, farmers lost their land to big collective farms.

THEY'RE COMING FOR THE COW NEXT WEEK.

OR, WE COULD EAT IT.

HMM....

Farmers who resisted were "liquidated."

FARMER

MRS. FARMER

The collective farms didn't produce as much as the old private ones, but Stalin's workers still had to eat.

WHAT WILL *WE* EAT?

NOT MY PROBLEM.

GRAIN

Millions of people starved to death in the fertile Ukraine between 1932 and 1933.

FOR COMRADE STALIN

HANDS OFF!

GRAIN

GRAIN

Stalin's industrial plans went better, but they had problems, too.

BRICKS

COAL

STEEL

FOOD

As things went wrong, instead of *backing off* like Lenin had (page 101), Stalin tried to control *more*, which led to more problems, and so on. Soon Stalin suspected *sabotage*.

He started *executing engineers*, which didn't help.

EVERYONE IS AGAINST ME!

A German right-wing crazy, Adolf Hitler, knew it, too.

"[PEOPLE] MORE READILY FALL VICTIM TO THE *BIG LIE* THAN THE SMALL LIE."

And in Depression-era Germany, where unemployment reached an unbearable *40%*, crazies thrived like infections in a weakened body.

IT'S THE CAPITALISTS!

IT'S THE JEWS!

IT'S THE BUSINESS CYCLE?

Hitler and his *National Socialist* party (*Nazi* for short) took power in early 1933. The Nazi program did have some socialist elements:

Benefits for workers (but no unions).

Public works programs, especially *highways*.

The "people's car" (*Volkswagen*) to drive on those highways.

HOSPITAL

REGIMENTED VACATIONS

But the nationalism came first. Hitler wanted a *rematch* of WWI, which brings us back to:

WORLD WAR II

The war started in 1939 and went global in 1941: First Hitler attacked the U.S.S.R., partly to get Russia's *oil*.

WHAT THE?

Then Japan attacked the U.S., also for oil, indirectly.

MAKES SENSE.

SEE, WE ATTACKED CHINA TO GET RESOURCES, BUT THAT PROVOKED EMBARGOES, SO NOW WE'RE RUNNING OUT OF OIL. THE NEAREST OIL IS IN THE DUTCH EAST INDIES (INDONESIA), BUT ATTACKING THERE WILL PROVOKE A CONFRONTATION WITH THE U.S., SO WE'RE ATTACKING THE U.S. *FIRST*.

Getting the U.S. on a war footing took some doing.

WHAT *HAPPENED* TO YOU?

THE DEPRESSION!

And the New Deal? FDR explained:

~~PWA~~
~~WPA~~
~~NYA~~
~~CCC~~

"DR. NEW DEAL" IS DONE; NOW THE COUNTRY'S UNDER THE TREATMENT OF "DR. WIN-THE-WAR."

Dr. Win-the-War *liked* big business. The unemployed disappeared into the factories and the army, and the American economy, idled for so long, showed what it could do.

Germany fell in early 1945; Japan not long after.

It is an age in which all the old admonitions appear to be outdated. "Make do." "Neither a borrower or a lender be." "Penny-wise, pound-foolish." "Waste not, want not." "A penny saved is a penny earned." "A fool and his money are soon parted." Just past the midmark of the 20th century, it looks as though all of our business forces are bent on getting everyone to do just the reverse. Borrow. Spend. Buy. Waste. Want.

—*Business Week* (1956)

GUNS
AND
BUTTER

(1945–1966)

THE POSTWAR WORLD WAS A MESS, AND RECENT HISTORY DIDN'T GIVE MUCH CAUSE FOR OPTIMISM.

| Keynes's *The Economic Consequences of the Peace* | | Great Depression | | Keynes's *General Theory* | | WWII begins |

| WWI begins | Mussolini takes power | | Ukraine famine | | Japan attacks China | |

| 1914 | 1919 | 1922 | 1930-39 | 1932-39 | 1936 | 1937 | 1939 |
| 1917 | | 1922-23 | 1929 | | 1933 | 1937 | 1945 |

Lenin takes power

Stocks crash

Hitler takes power

Great terror begins

German hyperinflation

FDR inaugurated

"[Europe is] a rubble heap, a charnel house, a breeding ground of pestilence and hate."
—Winston Churchill (1874-1965), prime minister of Britain during WWII, speaking after the war

BUT **WISE POLICIES** FIXED MANY PROBLEMS QUICKLY.

WISH I GOT TO SAY THAT MORE OFTEN.

WINNING THE PEACE

Far from being ravaged, the U.S. economy had been **pumped up** by the war.

American goods had to get to the rest of the world. But how would the rest of the world pay?

Harry Truman (1884-1972), who succeeded FDR as president when FDR died in 1945.

WE'LL *GIVE* THEM THE MONEY!

The famous **Marshall Plan** (1947) sent billions of dollars to Western Europe, former allies and former enemies alike.

UK
FRANCE

Also, the Marshall Plan money could be **spent**, not just sent back to pay off war debts, because WWII left less debt than WWI had. That was thanks to the Lend-Lease Act of 1941, another example of FDR's original thinking.

With lend-lease, the U.S. didn't lend its allies the money to buy ships, planes, and trucks—it lent them the **things themselves**.

WITHOUT THAT "SILLY, FOOLISH OLD DOLLAR SIGN!"

I.O.U. 5,000 TANKS - WINSTON

After the war:

WANT YOUR OBSOLETE TANKS BACK?

FORGET IT.

So nearly $50 billion worth of WWII "loans" didn't leave much debt.

133

The U.S. also pushed *international cooperation*.

The *United Nations* (1945) was a world government, but like the Continental Congress (page 57), it had (and has) no power to *tax*.

WHICH MEANS NO POWER.

The *World Bank* (1944) made loans for reconstruction.

The *General Agreement on Tariffs and Trade* (GATT; 1947) was an international forum to reach general agreements on tariffs and trade.

LOW TARIFFS AND LOTS OF TRADE!

The World Bank and the GATT were negotiated at the *Bretton Woods Conference* (1944), which also created a *managed money supply*. The dollar was exchangeable for gold (sort of).

SO I CAN TRADE PAPER DOLLARS FOR GOLD?

NOPE! YOU STILL CAN'T *OWN* GOLD!

GOLD WINDOW

And other countries' currencies were exchangeable for *dollars* at fixed rates.

FRANCS MARKS LIRA FRANCS

The *International Monetary Fund* (IMF; 1945) kept reserves to help with crises.

WE'RE ALMOST OUT OF DOLLARS!

BANK OF ENGLAND

HERE'S MORE!

IMF

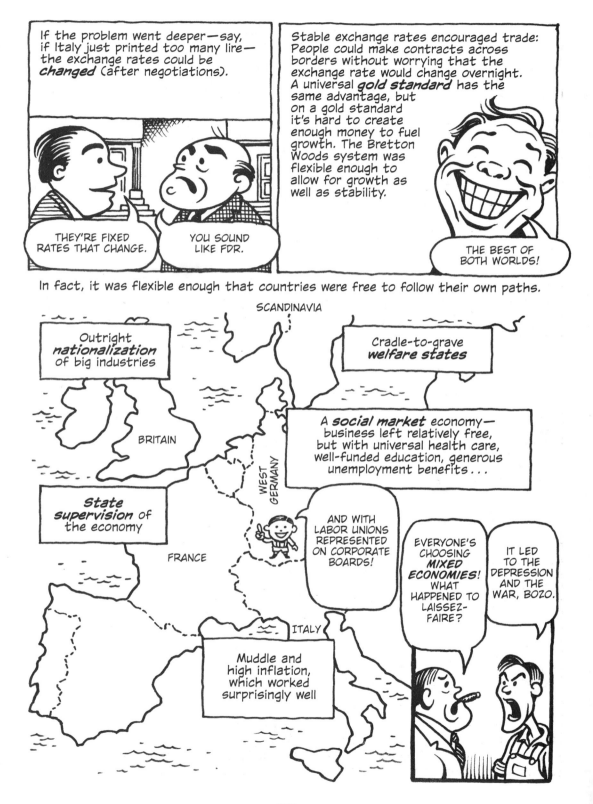

If the problem went deeper—say, if Italy just printed too many lire—the exchange rates could be **changed** (after negotiations).

THEY'RE FIXED RATES THAT CHANGE.

YOU SOUND LIKE FDR.

Stable exchange rates encouraged trade: People could make contracts across borders without worrying that the exchange rate would change overnight. A universal **gold standard** has the same advantage, but on a gold standard it's hard to create enough money to fuel growth. The Bretton Woods system was flexible enough to allow for growth as well as stability.

THE BEST OF BOTH WORLDS!

In fact, it was flexible enough that countries were free to follow their own paths.

SCANDINAVIA

Outright **nationalization** of big industries

Cradle-to-grave **welfare states**

BRITAIN

A **social market** economy—business left relatively free, but with universal health care, well-funded education, generous unemployment benefits . . .

WEST GERMANY

State supervision of the economy

AND WITH LABOR UNIONS REPRESENTED ON CORPORATE BOARDS!

FRANCE

EVERYONE'S CHOOSING **MIXED ECONOMIES**! WHAT HAPPENED TO LAISSEZ-FAIRE?

IT LED TO THE DEPRESSION AND THE WAR, BOZO.

ITALY

Muddle and high inflation, which worked surprisingly well

THE COLD WAR

All the American generosity and engagement we've just seen *excluded* someone.

The U.S. and the U.S.S.R. had *allied* during WWII, but postwar, that fell apart fast. The Soviets set up puppet Stalinist governments in the countries they'd occupied at the end of the war, while the Americans sabotaged communist movements in the countries *they'd* occupied.

ENEMIES OF THE STATE

ENEMIES OF THE PEOPLE

Within a very short time, the U.S. was practically at *war* with the U.S.S.R., minus the actual fighting.

IT'S A *COLD WAR!*

1947: Truman commits the U.S. to "containing" communism.

1948: The Soviets blockade West Berlin; the U.S. supplies the city by air (!) until the Soviets give up.

1949: The Soviets build an atomic bomb.

1949: Mao's communists take over China, except Taiwan, where Chiang Kai-shek holds out.

1950: The U.S. and Communist China go to war in Korea.

Meanwhile, back in America, people went about their business.

WHAT ELSE IS THERE TO DO?

And business had *never been better*.

THE LONG BOOM

At first Americans were worried about the post-war economy.

WITHOUT ALL THE WAR SPENDING, WON'T THE **DEPRESSION** COME BACK?

But the economy barely missed a beat.

One reason: War workers had been **well paid** during the war (because the government said they **had** to be).

All that pay, chasing after a restricted supply of consumer goods, could have produced serious **inflation**.

TWENTY DOLLARS!

FORTY!

NINETY!

But a giant government bureaucracy had **controlled** prices during the war.

$15

That pretty much forced people to **save** their money, to the tune of an incredible $230 billion by 1945 (by comparison, the **entire federal budget** in 1939 was less than $10 billion). After the war, people started **spending** those savings.

137

Even after the first flood of wartime savings was spent, the economy kept zooming, because people had **purchasing power**.

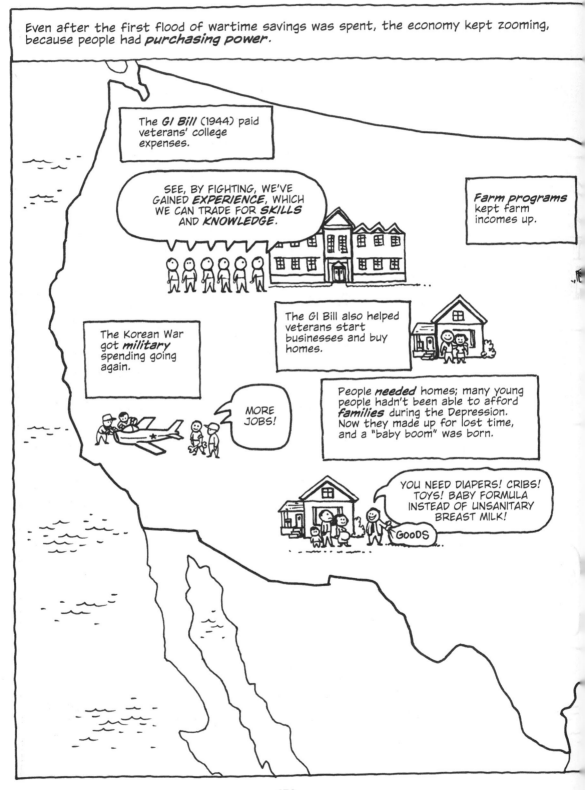

The **GI Bill** (1944) paid veterans' college expenses.

SEE, BY FIGHTING, WE'VE GAINED **EXPERIENCE**, WHICH WE CAN TRADE FOR **SKILLS** AND **KNOWLEDGE**.

Farm programs kept farm incomes up.

The GI Bill also helped veterans start businesses and buy homes.

The Korean War got **military** spending going again.

MORE JOBS!

People **needed** homes; many young people hadn't been able to afford **families** during the Depression. Now they made up for lost time, and a "baby boom" was born.

YOU NEED DIAPERS! CRIBS! TOYS! BABY FORMULA INSTEAD OF UNSANITARY BREAST MILK!

GOODS

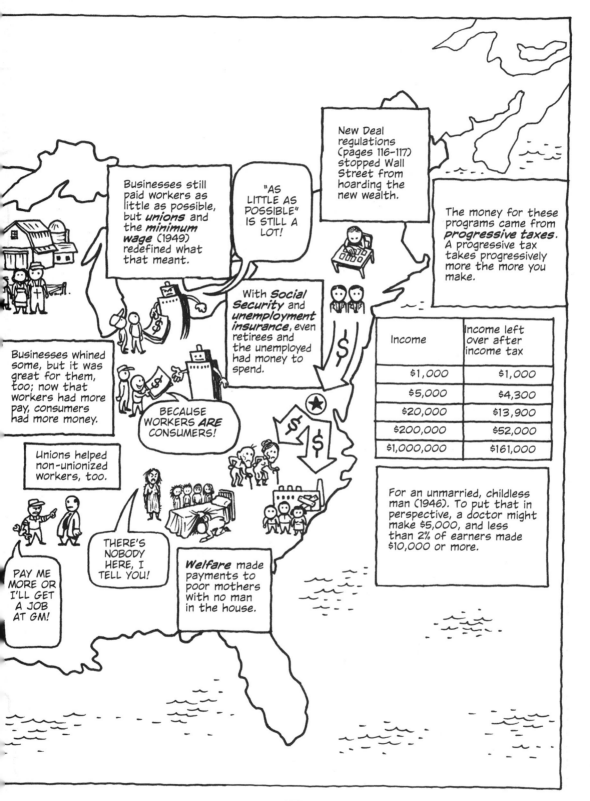

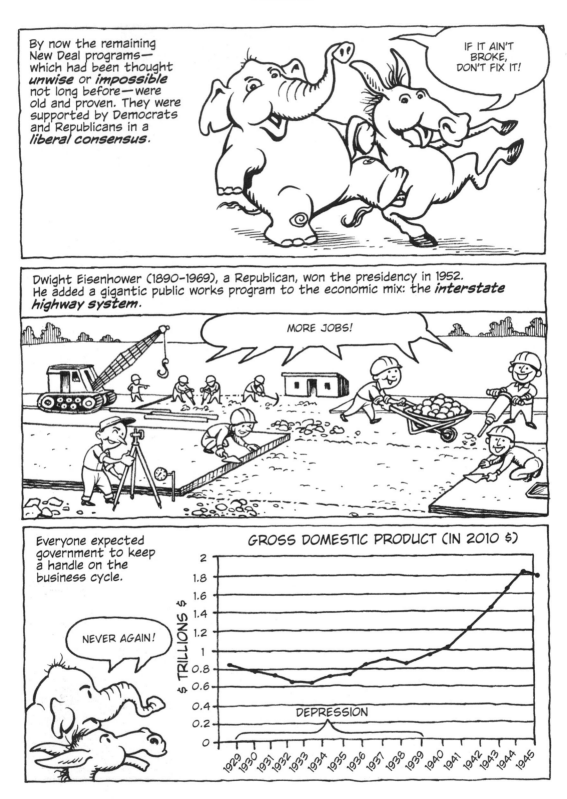

By now the remaining New Deal programs—which had been thought **unwise** or **impossible** not long before—were old and proven. They were supported by Democrats and Republicans in a *liberal consensus*.

IF IT AIN'T BROKE, DON'T FIX IT!

Dwight Eisenhower (1890–1969), a Republican, won the presidency in 1952. He added a gigantic public works program to the economic mix: the *interstate highway system*.

MORE JOBS!

Everyone expected government to keep a handle on the business cycle.

NEVER AGAIN!

GROSS DOMESTIC PRODUCT (IN 2010 $)

$ TRILLIONS $

2
1.8
1.6
1.4
1.2
1
0.8
0.6
0.4
0.2
0

DEPRESSION

1929 1930 1931 1932 1933 1934 1935 1936 1937 1938 1939 1940 1941 1942 1943 1944 1945

MANAGING THE BUSINESS CYCLE MEANT TRACKING IT. THE GOVERNMENT STARTED COLLECTING REAMS OF STATISTICS THAT WE STILL USE TODAY. THEY'RE NOT ENTIRELY RELIABLE, BUT THEY'RE BETTER THAN NOTHING.

MONEY SUPPLY EXPORTS GDP NNP PPI UNEMPLOYMENT TMI MPC CPI IMPORTS GNP MPS

The big statistic: **gross domestic product** (GDP), which is all the new goods and services sold by everyone.

THE WHOLE OUTPUT OF THE ECONOMY!

Up until the 1990s the government stressed **gross national product** (GNP), which is GDP plus Americans' income from overseas, minus money sent overseas.

GDP counts only **final** goods and services, to avoid double-counting.

25¢
50¢
FLOUR
BREAD
$1

Total contribution to GDP: $1, not $1.75

As long as you buy something, GDP goes up (no matter what you're buying)....

BAD FOR GDP

GOOD FOR GDP

UNLESS IT'S ILLEGAL.

Counted in GDP

BEER

Not counted in GDP

GDP COUNTS ONLY **MONEY TRANSACTIONS**. A FOREST DOESN'T COUNT IN GDP UNLESS WE CUT IT DOWN.

For that matter, if we cook our own food, clean our own houses, and care for our own kids, it **doesn't** register in GDP. If we eat at restaurants, pay people to clean our houses, and send our kids to day care, it **does**. So GDP can grow **horizontally**, where the same amount of work is being done, but GDP rises because the work has moved to the money economy.

GDP HAS TO BE ADJUSTED FOR CHANGES IN **PRICE** SO WE KNOW WHETHER WE'RE GETTING MORE STUFF OR PAYING MORE FOR THE SAME STUFF.

$$\frac{5\% \text{ GDP GROWTH IN DOLLAR TERMS ADJUSTED FOR INFLATION}}{= 2\% \text{ GROWTH IN } REAL \text{ GDP}}$$

WHEN I TALK ABOUT GDP, I MEAN **REAL** GDP.

IT'S WORTH STRESSING THAT GDP COUNTS THE COSTS OF THINGS, NOT THE BENEFITS WE GET FROM THEM. FOR INSTANCE, CHEAP TAP WATER BARELY COUNTS IN GDP.

IF WE HAVE TO SWITCH TO EXPENSIVE **BOTTLED** WATER, GDP GOES UP, BUT IT'S HARD TO SEE HOW WE'RE BETTER OFF.

In the 1950s, memories of the Depression were still raw; it made sense that keeping GDP rising became **the** economic priority.

And people knew how to do it:

SPEND MORE!

KEYNES

SAMUELSON AND THE SYNTHESIS

Where did these economists come from? Economists had to be **trained** in Keynes's ideas, but Keynes's *General Theory* (page 121) wasn't really accessible to beginners.

Enter a young American economist, Paul Samuelson (1915-2009). His book *Economics: An Introductory Analysis* (1948) conveyed Keynes's ideas in clear, engaging prose.

"IN 1932 PEOPLE WALKED THE STREET WITHOUT WORK; IN 1929 AND 1946 THE SAME PEOPLE HAD PROSPEROUS JOBS. THE ANSWER IS NOT IN THEM."

ECONOMICS

Samuelson used Keynes's ideas for **macroeconomics**— the big picture.

Unlike Keynes, Samuelson kept neoclassical ideas (page 67) to explain **microeconomics**— the small stuff like how single markets operate, how individual firms behave, and how consumers fill shopping baskets to get the most satisfaction for their money.

DEMAND SUPPLY

It wasn't really a synthesis, though: Samuelson laid Keynes's ideas on top of the neoclassical world, with a **fudge factor** in between.

DEMAND SUPPLY

MMM, FUDGE.

The combination was called neoclassical Keynesian economics, or the **neoclassical synthesis**.

STILL, SAMUELSON'S *ECONOMICS* WAS THE TEMPLATE FOR PRETTY MUCH EVERY BASIC ECON TEXT THAT FOLLOWED. AS OF 2011, THE BOOK IS IN ITS 19TH EDITION.

That was achievement enough, but Samuelson had published **another** influential work the year before. *Foundations of Economic Analysis* (1947) restated **all** of economics as **pure math**.

FOUNDATIONS

By providing a clear explanation of Keynes's ideas, as well as all the complexity the most clever scholar could want, Samuelson firmly established Keynes in mainstream economic theory.

ECONOMICS

FOUNDA-TIONS

SPEND MORE!

THE AMERICAN DREAM

With an economy managed by Keynesians, the old boom-and-bust became more of a boom-and-pause.

REAL GDP (IN 2000 $)

As the poor got richer, the very rich didn't (thanks to high taxes). Many rich people accepted the new rules with good grace.

"THERE IS NO RATIONAL JUSTIFICATION FOR MY FAMILY HAVING THE AMOUNT OF MONEY THAT IT HAS.... THE ONLY HONEST THING TO SAY IN DEFENSE OF IT IS THAT WE LIKE HAVING THE MONEY AND THE PRESENT SOCIAL SYSTEM ALLOWS US TO KEEP IT."

Steven Rockefeller, great-grandson of John D.

Some rich folks still got misty-eyed about the 1920s, and even insisted that the Depression hadn't been so bad before FDR ruined everything. Here's former president Hoover, in his 1951 memoirs, talking about the Depression.

"MANY PERSONS LEFT THEIR JOBS FOR THE MORE PROFITABLE ONE OF SELLING APPLES."

HERBERT HOOVER, LADIES AND GENTLEMEN! A BIG HAND!

Either way, the rich were *losing power*. They didn't even control the corporations they still owned; by now most big corporations had too many stockholders for one person to have much of a voice.

I OWN 0.07% OF THIS COMPANY AND I THINK —

SCRAM.

Also, postwar companies were *complex*; few stockholders could be bothered to keep track. So stockholders mostly knew what management *told* them. For that matter, the same was true of *directors*, who met only a few times a year.

That left management somewhat autonomous. Big corporations wound up controlled by their managers— that is, by their *own employees*.

"Blue-collar" worker

"White-collar" worker

WE'RE BOTH JUST WORKERS!

By the 1950s, with the poor getting richer, and the very rich becoming less relevant, America seemed to be turning into one big *middle class*.

"*The United States, the world's largest capitalist country, has from the standpoint of the distribution of wealth come closest to the ideal of prosperity for all in a classless society.*" —Richard Nixon (1913-1994), Eisenhower's vice president (1959)

Economic growth, and reasonably widespread distribution of the benefits, had solved all sorts of problems.

ANYONE WHO WORKS HARD AND STAYS SOBER CAN MAKE IT!

But some problems *can't* be solved by growth.

LITTLE BOXES: The Suburbs

For instance, all those new homes were built mainly in suburbs. People didn't so much *move* to the suburbs as get *pulled* there by *subsidies*.

MORTGAGE TAX BREAKS! MORTGAGE GUARANTEES! FREE HIGHWAYS!

And the homes were ready for them, in mass-produced developments.

SALES

These developments were called "towns," but real towns develop *organically*, by the individual and collective decisions of many people choosing where to put their homes, how big to build them, where to build the school . . .

Postwar developments were *planned* (often *badly* planned), with no public space to hold a protest or a parade, no variety, plus–since houses in a tract all cost the same–*economic segregation*, that is, separation of rich and poor . . .

which wasn't the only type of segregation.

I'M HERE FOR MY HOUSE.

SALES

GO AWAY!

Still, tract housing was a big step up for a generation that had grown up in boxcars and barracks, and with all the subsidies, it was irrational *not* to move to the suburbs. The new middle class left the cities, taking the *tax base* with them.

SUBURBANITES *USE* THE CITY, BUT THEY DON'T PAY TAXES TO *SUPPORT* IT.

ANOTHER SUBSIDY!

Cities did try to lure the middle class back. One common bad idea:

WE'LL MAKE OUR CITY *CAR FRIENDLY!*

Between 1950 and 1953, New York City spent $143 million on schools, $4 million on libraries, $70 million on hospitals, and *$172 million* on highways, whether they made sense or not. Other cities went further.

SHOP MART

Cars, parking, and roads use up a lot of land. Towns and cities had to *spread out*.

1930s

STORE   SCHOOL   GAS

1950s

THE MORE WE ACCOMMODATE CARS, THE MORE WE *NEED* CARS!

PARKING   CARS 4 SALE   AUTO STORE   OIL & LUBE   SCHOOL   TIRES   GAS   GAS

So people bought more cars...

which needed more highways and parking spaces...

so cities sprawled more...

Mass transit is less economical when cities sprawl. And just for good measure, GM, Firestone Tire, and some oil companies bought dozens of *trolley lines* and ran them into the ground.

I GUESS IT'S TIME TO FREELY CHOOSE TO BUY CARS.

BIG GOVERNMENT

THE COMPANIES THAT PULLED OFF THE TRICK WITH THE TROLLEY LINES WERE CONVICTED, BUT THEY WERE LET OFF WITH A SLAP ON THE WRIST, WHICH SHOWED HOW TIMES WERE *CHANGING.*

One big change: By the 1950s, government was becoming *bureaucratic.* Bureaucracies tend to do what's easiest, which often means giving in to *pressure.*

GIMME!

GIMME!

GIMME!

GIMME!

GIMME!

Pressure—legal political contributions, lobbying expenses, PR campaigns, bribery—cost *money*, so:

The more money a special interest had, the more clout it had in Washington.

The more favors it got, the more money it had.

The more clout it had, the more favors it could get.

Meanwhile, programs that served people who *needed* the help tended to wither.

IF WE HAD ANY CLOUT, WE COULD DIRECT SOME OF THAT FEDERAL MONEY OUR WAY.

IF WE HAD MONEY, WE'D HAVE CLOUT.

The special interest with the most clout was **big business**, which was very cozy with government by the 1950s.

WE'RE WAR BUDDIES!

AREN'T YOU SUPPOSED TO BE, YOU KNOW, **FIGHTING** OR SOMETHING?

In the Korean War, a giant military joined the lovefest. This wasn't the first big war machine the U.S. had created, but it was the first to **stick around** when the war was over.

?

One group of people ran the whole shebang...

JOHN J. MCCLOY

assistant secretary of war, chairman of Chase Bank, president of the World Bank, and high commissioner for Germany

CHARLES WILSON

secretary of defense and chairman of GM

DOUGLAS MACARTHUR

general of the army and chairman of Remington Rand

ROBERT MCNAMARA

secretary of defense, head of the World Bank, and CEO of Ford

which is more evidence of what we saw on page 81: Big corporations resemble government departments, to the point that running one is a lot like running the other.

Bureaucrat

Executive

Big business, the government, and the military all shared a **common goal**. Charles Wilson, chairman of GM and secretary of defense, had a name for it:

THE "PERMANENT WAR ECONOMY"

In 1947, the Pentagon said it would take 150 Hiroshima-size nukes to beat the U.S.S.R., if it came to that.

150 HIROSHIMA BOMBS = 3 MEGATONS TOTAL

SOUNDS ABOUT RIGHT.

WE CAN AFFORD THAT.

By 1960, the U.S. had built the equivalent of 100,000 Hiroshima-size bombs.

WHAT WE NEED:
1. MORE
2. MORE
3. MORE

Every year, it seemed, the military "needed" just about as much firepower as industry could supply.

THEY HAVE MORE!

THEY HAVE MORE!

One reason: In World War II, the government got into the habit of giving out **cost-plus contracts**—suppliers were paid their costs plus a **guaranteed profit**. Many big businesses came to depend on military spending.

Technology often depended on military spending, too; a lot of military research in rocketry, aircraft, and electronics *spilled over* into the rest of the economy. By 1962, the U.S. had spent *three times* more for electronics in missiles than for electronics in TVs.

EVEN THE *SPRAY CAN* WAS A MILITARY SPILLOVER!

But we saw on page 93 how an arms race led to a world war; that nearly happened again, more than once, with consequences that don't even bear thinking about.

On the other hand, all this military spending meant profits and jobs, so there wasn't as much protest as might have been expected. And what protest there was often wasn't *heard*.

BIG AND BLAND: The Postwar Media

The logic of economies of scale we saw on page 76—*rising initial costs* and *falling per-unit costs*—applied to *newspapers* as much as steel.

Newspaper press, 1750s

Newspaper press, 1950s

WE NEED TO SELL A *LOT* OF CHEAP PAPERS TO PAY FOR THE EXPENSIVE PRESS!

By the 1950s, an entire *city* might provide enough readers for only one big paper.

PREWAR NEWSSTAND

DEMOCRAT NEWS | REPUBLICAN CHRONICLE | DAILY SOCIALIST

EVENING RIGHT-WING APOLOGIST | COMMIE TIMES | THE TOTALLY UNHINGED MORNING POST

POSTWAR NEWSSTAND

DAILY SNORE | DAILY SNORE | DAILY SNORE

DAILY SNORE | DAILY SNORE | DAILY SNORE

Since a big paper is, by definition, a big business, more people got their information from big business.

And that was nothing compared to a *new* medium.

HELLO!

Television spread like wildfire after WWII.

"If the use of leisure hours is confined to looking at TV for a few extra hours a day, we will deteriorate as a people." —Eleanor Roosevelt, former First Lady (1958)

And talk about concentrated ownership: For decades, starting in the 1940s, there were only three TV networks for the whole **country**.

AND THAT'S THE WAY IT IS!

IT IS!

Broadcast TV isn't exactly in business to serve its audience (the audience doesn't pay). Rather, it's in business to serve its audience **to advertisers**.

PAYS $

SHOWS ADS

PAYS $$

Angering advertisers would be a dumb business plan, so TV (and radio, magazines, and newspapers for that matter) often *censors itself*.

William Shirer, legendary journalist fired in 1947 because CBS worried that an advertiser *might* object to his reporting.

So news, information, and opinion—to some degree culture itself—became a *one-way flow*.

SANITIZED FOR YOUR PROTECTION

People could dissent, but that didn't matter as it once had. Look at it this way: If you've been angry enough to yell at the TV...

@#&*@#!!

TO BE *SECURE*, WE NEED MORE WEAPONS!

maybe others were yelling, too. Maybe everyone was. But so what? Nobody could *hear* anybody else.

@#⚡*!! @#⚡!! @#⚡*@!! @#⚡8!!

@#&*⚡!! @##⚡8*!! @#⚡@*⚡!!

That *voicelessness* may help explain the postwar spread of *political apathy*. Even grave political questions started to come down to who looked good on TV....

ELECTION 1960

NEW FRONTIERS AND GREAT SOCIETIES: JFK and LBJ

Which brings us to 1961, when President Dwight Eisenhower left office with a **warning**:

"THIS CONJUNCTION OF AN IMMENSE MILITARY ESTABLISHMENT AND A LARGE ARMS INDUSTRY IS NEW IN THE AMERICAN EXPERIENCE.... THE POTENTIAL FOR THE DISASTROUS RISE OF MISPLACED POWER EXISTS AND WILL PERSIST."

Eisenhower **named** the agglomeration of power we described on pages 150–151.

IT'S THE *MILITARY-INDUSTRIAL COMPLEX!*

The new president, Democrat John F. Kennedy (1917–1963), brought some **vision** and **energy** back to government.

HELP THE POOR! SEND A MAN TO THE MOON! FIX CIVIL RIGHTS! GET OUR HANDS DIRTY!

JFK's administration saw the "discovery of the poor," when the government noticed that there were still poor people in America.

BUT A RISING TIDE FLOATS ALL BOATS!

DON'T *GOT* A BOAT.

Kennedy was killed in 1963; his programs were pushed through by his successor, Lyndon Johnson (1908–1973), an old FDR man.

LBJ won the 1964 election in a landslide.

Medicare (health care for old people)

Medicaid (health care for poor people)

A "war on poverty" (reasonably successful, actually)

Attempts to deal with the consequences of *growth*, like pollution and sprawl

Head Start

Sesame Street

NOW IT'S TIME FOR *MY* PROGRAM, THE GREAT SOCIETY!

The Great Society would be expensive, but the money was there. JFK had stimulated the economy with a *tax cut*...

and Keynesian economists played the economy like an instrument, keeping inflation low and employment high.

In 1965, *Time* magazine put Keynes, dead nearly 20 years, on the cover, saying:

"The men who formulate the nation's economic policies have used Keynesian principles not only to avoid the violent cycles of prewar days but to produce a phenomenal economic growth and to achieve remarkably stable prices."
—*Time* (December 31, 1965)

But 1965 was also the *last* year the U.S. economy worked like it was supposed to. To explain why, we need to catch up to the rest of the world....

Without markets, it was hard to tell what people wanted.

DID YOU BRING US WASHING MACHINES?

MOTORBIKES?

REFRIGERATORS? CARS?

NO! I BROUGHT *MORE TRACTORS!* ISN'T THAT GREAT?

Still, the Soviets had food, clothes, and medical care. Even better, Stalin finally died in 1953. Under his successor, Nikita Khrushchev, people could breathe more freely.

NOT *TOO* MUCH MORE FREELY!

The end of the Hungarian Revolution of 1956.

AND A TOP-DOWN SOCIETY CAN DO *BIG* PROJECTS WELL. THE FIRST SATELLITE, THE FIRST HUMAN IN SPACE, AND THE FIRST UNMANNED MOON LANDING WERE ALL *COMMUNIST* ACHIEVEMENTS.

"WE WILL BURY YOU!"

So the "communist world" still stood toe-to-toe with the "free world." Their rivalry played out in the *rest* of the world, called:

THE "THIRD WORLD"

Let's backtrack to the end of WWII, when most of Europe's colonies started to win their independence. The world got more **complicated**.

PAKISTANIS?

CAMBODIANS?

UPPER VOLTANS?

The U.S. dominated this new world, but many Americans didn't know much about it.

"We will lift Shanghai up and up, ever up, until it's just like Kansas City."
— Senator Kenneth Wherry of Nebraska (1940)

For instance, most of the world was still stuck on the farm and needed **land reform** more than anything, but . . .

LAND REFORM IS **COMMUNIST**! YOU HAVE TO RESPECT THE LANDLORD'S PRIVATE PROPERTY!

LANDLORD

WE'D RESPECT PROPERTY IF WE **HAD** SOME.

Americans who **did** understand such things were **purged** from government.

YOU SAID MAO WOULD WIN IN CHINA!

YES, I WARNED THAT . . .

Joseph McCarthy

SO IT'S **YOUR FAULT** MAO WON!

WHAT?

American foreign policy became scandalously **simpleminded**.

ANY COMMUNIST SUCCESS ANYWHERE WILL MEAN SOVIET TAKEOVER **EVERYWHERE**! JUST LIKE KNOCKING OVER **ONE** DOMINO MAKES THEM **ALL** FALL!

VERY IMPRESSIVE. YOU UNDERSTAND **DOMINOES**.

The worry was that true democracies might let communists come to power.

STRONG ANTICOMMUNISTS ARE BETTER.

159

So the sort of American generosity we saw on page 133 sometimes went to *dictators*, which dovetailed with the needs of *big corporations*.

DEMOCRACIES TRY TO KEEP MY RESOURCES FOR THEM- SELVES!

YOUR RESOURCES?

And "anticommunism" became, in part, a new name for an old story: the government providing muscle for big business.

I CAN PLAY WITH MY SOLDIERS AGAIN!

For example, the Anglo-Persian Oil Company (today's BP) had cheated Iran out of its oil for decades; in 1951, Iran's elected prime minister, Mohammad Mossadeq, *nationalized* Iran's oil, which made other oil companies nervous.

OURS!

In 1953, Mossadeq was toppled with CIA help, and Shah Mohammad Reza Pahlavi took over.

YOURS!

DAMN STRAIGHT!

Once you've installed a dictator, you can't just let people remove him, so the U.S. wound up *committed* to dictators all over the world, including a place called South Vietnam. By the time LBJ took office, that regime was near collapse thanks to insurgents called the Viet Cong, many of whom were land-reforming communists.

President Johnson cared about his Great Society, not some farmers on the other side of the world, but a commitment is a commitment.

MAKE THIS PROBLEM GO AWAY.

U.S.A.: BLANK CHECK PAY TO ARMY L.B.J.

The increased military spending hit an economy going full blast and started to crowd out other spending; in 1966, inflation hit 3%, which was high in those days.

LBJ raised taxes to cool things down, but it was too little too late, and anyway, the big, permanent military turned out to be better at spending money than winning wars.

YOU NEED **MORE**?

Which brings us back to page 156, and an economy that wasn't working like it was supposed to.

INTEREST RATES

IMPORTS

EXPORTS

BORROWING

GOVERNMENT SPENDING

CONSUMER SPENDING/SAVING

TAX REVENUE

MULTIPLIER

UNEMPLOYMENT

$VELOCITY

CONSUMER CONFIDENCE

$ SUPPLY

The Great Society fizzled as the money went to a war that wouldn't end.

YOU NEED **MORE**?

REALLY, THE ECONOMY WOULD NEVER BE THE SAME AGAIN.

An industrial system which uses forty per cent of the world's resources to supply less than six per cent of the world's population could be called efficient only if it obtained strikingly successful results in terms of human happiness, well-being, culture, peace, and harmony. I do not need to dwell on the fact that the American system fails to do this, or that there are not the slightest prospects that it could do so if *only* it achieved a higher rate of growth of production.

—E. F. Schumacher, *Small Is Beautiful* (1973)

CHAPTER 6

THE
ERA OF
LIMITS

(1966–1980)

Until the end of the 1960s, the economic news wasn't all bad.

INFLATION IS HIGH BECAUSE **EMPLOYMENT** IS HIGH. PEOPLE HAVE SO MUCH INCOME THAT THEY'RE TRYING TO BUY MORE THAN THE ECONOMY CAN PRODUCE.

IT'S **DEMAND-PULL INFLATION**.

In fact, the trade-off between inflation and unemployment had never been clearer.

INFLATION VS. UNEMPLOYMENT, 1963-1968

In years when unemployment was low, inflation was high.

In years when unemployment was high, inflation was low.

Then America started getting **stagflation** — high inflation and high unemployment together.

INFLATION VS UNEMPLOYMENT, 1969-1975

WHAT. THE. HECK.

The inflation couldn't be demand-pull inflation, because there was clearly slack capacity in the economy (all the unemployed who could have been working).

Stagflation wasn't just an academic problem; it was a **policy** problem.

INFLATION'S HIGH, BUT WE KNOW HOW TO DEAL WITH THAT: REIN IN THE ECONOMY.

BUT THAT WORSENS UNEMPLOYMENT, AND UNEMPLOYMENT'S HIGH, TOO.

SO? WE CAN CUT UNEMPLOYMENT — JUST PUMP UP THE ECONOMY.

BUT THAT WORSENS INFLATION.

WAIT A MINUTE . . .

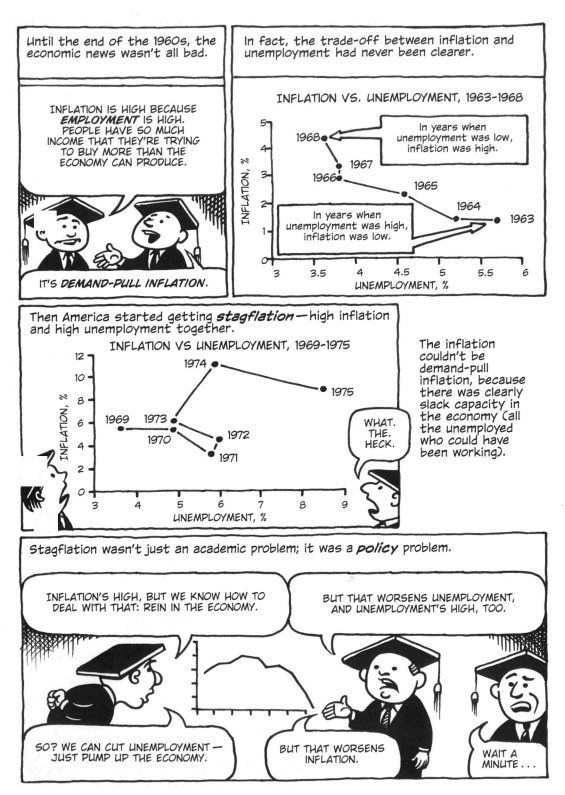

It was understandable that economists were confused by stagflation. After all, in mainstream economics, price was set by supply and demand.

> FOR INFLATION TO OCCUR, THERE HAS TO BE TOO LITTLE SUPPLY OR TOO MUCH DEMAND. BUT NEITHER IS HAPPENING!

But here's another explanation for inflation: People had come to **expect** it.

Prices rise.

Everyone expects more inflation.

Businesses demand higher prices while workers demand higher wages.

This idea was hard to express with math, and since the 1940s, economists had built a huge structure of mathematical models, especially for microeconomics. Each model fit rigorously with previous models, which fit with previous ones, all the way down to the *microfoundations*—the fundamental assumptions behind the model, some of which we saw on page 71.

DEMAND   SUPPLY

Remember, though, that microfoundations describe an *imaginary, ideal universe*, so they're a shaky base to build on if you're trying to describe the real world.

But many mainstream economists sort of forgot that.

"MATHEMATICAL ANALYSIS IS NOT ONE OF MANY WAYS OF DOING ECONOMIC THEORY; IT IS THE ONLY WAY. ECONOMIC THEORY IS MATHEMATICAL ANALYSIS. EVERYTHING ELSE IS JUST PICTURES AND TALK."

Robert Lucas (1937–), American economist

WHAT ABOUT PICTURES THAT TALK?

Keynes had never really *fit* on this rigorous structure, so when Keynesian policies started to stumble...

BUT MY IDEAS WORKED FOR MORE THAN *THIRTY YEARS!*

PICTURES AND TALK!

By the late 1960s, many mainstream economists were living in a world of *pure theory*, where it was hard to even *think* about ideas that couldn't be expressed with math.

SEE, THE HYPERPLANE SEPARATES THE INDIFFERENCE CURVE FROM THE TRANSFORMATION CURVE.

"The [economic] model is a work of art, freely composed within the constraints of a particular art form, namely the logical binding together of propositions. In this bounded freedom, it resembles any other art form: the sonnet, the symphony, the cabinet maker's or architect's conception...."
—George L. S. Shackle (1903–1992), English economist

For that matter, if businesses could raise their prices based on expectations, they must have had some *power* to set their prices. Mainstream economics *excluded* that possibility, but other economists had been studying it; let's take a break to look at *nonmainstream economics*.
(Or, skip ahead to page 174 if you don't care so much about theory.)

COMPETING MONOPOLIES

Consider **advertising**. Until recently, most economists didn't think much about it. When they did think about it, they thought:

> IT PERFORMS A **SERVICE**: IT LETS US KNOW WHAT WE CAN SPEND OUR MONEY ON.

10% OFF!

NEW DEVICE!

BOOKS

ECO NO MIX

ECO NO MIX

THE NEW BESTSELLER IS IN!

> THAT'S SOMETIMES TRUE. BUT TODAY, MCDONALD'S ADS DON'T INFORM US THAT MCDONALD'S HAS BURGERS FOR SALE. WE **KNOW** THAT. AND WE **KNOW** WHAT THEY TASTE LIKE.

But McDonald's spends $1.6 billion a year on **something**. That something is an **image** that has little to do with the drab reality of fried meat.

> FUN! CLOWNS! SONGS!

In the 1930s, the American economist Edward Chamberlin and British economist Joan Robinson pointed out that this sort of **branding** can make identical or nearly identical goods **seem** different.

REALITY

SOAP   SOAP   SOAP

IMAGE

DOVE   IRISH SPRING   LEVER 2000

> EVERY BRAND IS A GOVERNMENT-PROTECTED **MONOPOLY**. YOU CAN MAKE AND SELL COLA, BUT IF YOU CALL IT COKE®, YOU'RE GOING TO JAIL.

SUGAR

BATTERY ACID

Coke

> MONOPOLIES HAVE THE **POWER** TO CHARGE MORE. NEXT TIME YOU'RE IN THE DRUGSTORE, CHECK OUT HOW MUCH LESS GENERIC ACETAMINOPHEN, PYRITHIONE ZINC SHAMPOO, AND LORATADINE COST THAN THE EXACT SAME THINGS WITH BRANDS ADDED (TYLENOL®, HEAD & SHOULDERS®, AND CLARITIN®, RESPECTIVELY).

Rx   PHARMA

This means that today, competition doesn't always work the way it did on page 23. Rather, companies try to carve out monopolies, which lets them **set their prices** to some degree.

IT'S **MONOPOLISTIC COMPETITION.**

A FORM OF **IMPERFECT COMPETITION.**

Edward Chamberlin

Joan Robinson

Another way to look at it: Here's a free-market explanation for the high price of **diamonds**.

THE SUPPLY OF DIAMONDS IS LOW, **RELATIVE TO THE DEMAND,** SO THE PRICE IS HIGH.

DEMAND   SUPPLY

PRICE

QUANTITY

Alfred Marshall

But diamonds aren't really all that rare: The supply is restricted because the mines are owned by an **oligopoly** dominated by the South African corporation De Beers.

Demand is high partly because these ideas are part of our culture:

- A marriage proposal isn't real without a diamond ring.
- The ring should cost two months' salary.
- Diamonds are heirlooms and shouldn't be sold.

Ideas that originated in **advertising**, paid for by De Beers.

So **supply** is what De Beers wants to sell, while **demand** is, to some degree, what De Beers can convince us to buy.

WE CONTROL THE HORIZONTAL.

WE CONTROL THE VERTICAL.

DEMAND   SUPPLY

PRICE

QUANTITY

So is that an exception, or is it the rule? Well, on page 90 we saw that many markets are dominated by oligopolies, which have some control over supply.

"WE HAVE A SAYING AT THIS COMPANY. OUR COMPETITORS ARE OUR FRIENDS, AND OUR CUSTOMERS ARE OUR ENEMIES." —JAMES RANDALL, PRESIDENT OF ARCHER DANIELS MIDLAND (1990s)

And demand? Well...

BUY!!
BUY
BUY!
Buy!
BUY
BUY
NOW!
BUY ME
BUY
BUY!

THE EMBARRASSMENT OF RICHES: Galbraith

In *The Affluent Society* (1958), the economist John Kenneth Galbraith pointed out that nobody would bother with expensive ads just to sell us what we already wanted.

RELENTLESS ADVERTISING MAKES SENSE ONLY FOR THINGS WE NEED TO BE **PERSUADED** TO WANT.

4 OUT OF 5 DOCTORS AGREE. – FOOD CURES HUNGER

DON'T LET THIS BE YOU – *WEAR CLOTHES*

DOESN'T *YOUR* FAMILY DESERVE... SHELTER?

So instead of seeing the economy entirely like *this*...

WIDGET WORKS

We want something.

Business makes it.

We buy it and are satisfied.

Galbraith saw parts of it like *this*:

WIDGET WORKS

BUY!

We start out satisfied.

Business makes something...

and advertises it.

We want it, buy it, and are satisfied (for now).

This is a sensible use of society's resources.

This, not so much.

SATISFYING PEOPLE'S WANTS IS GOOD!

ADS CREATE A WANT → WHICH IS SATISFIED BY BUYING A PRODUCT ← THE PRODUCT PAYS FOR MORE ADS →

Not to mention how, after WWII, the richest nation in history started eating ton after ton of *cheap crud*.

"*More die in the United States of too much food than too little. Where the population was once thought to press upon the food supply, now the food supply presses relentlessly on the population.*" — John Kenneth Galbraith (1958)

THE SHEER PERVASIVENESS OF THIS PRESSURE TO CONSUME MAY EXPLAIN WHY AFTER WWII WE STARTED TO REFER TO OURSELVES AS **CONSUMERS** RATHER THAN, SAY, **WORKERS** OR **CITIZENS**. ON SOME LEVEL WE MAY HAVE *INTERNALIZED* THE IDEA THAT CONSUMING WAS OUR MAIN JOB.

We definitely internalized the idea that privately produced consumer goods are more important than anything, even the *public* sector.

$10 million for underwear (really!): a perfectly sensible use of society's resources

$10 million to repair a school: a scandalous waste of society's resources

As early as the 1950s, the public sector was *deteriorating*, to the point that people couldn't even fully enjoy their private goods: A big pothole would shake your spine no matter how good your shock absorbers were.

WE GET "*PRIVATE AFFLUENCE AND PUBLIC SQUALOR*"!

Now we can answer a question that has always bothered me—why we **celebrate** when people buy more cars and **despair** when people buy more health care. The answer is that we've internalized big business's point of view.

> IF YOU SPEND YOUR MONEY STAYING HEALTHY, YOU WON'T HAVE MONEY TO BUY MY CARS!

Imagine if it were different.

> DETROIT RELEASED SALES FIGURES TODAY INDICATING THAT THE **COST OF TRANSPORTATION** INCREASED, BURDENING THE REST OF THE ECONOMY.

NEWS

ANYWAY, WE STARTED THIS DISCUSSION BY TALKING ABOUT HOW BIG BUSINESS HAS THE POWER TO SET PRICES. I DON'T THINK ROBINSON, CHAMBERLIN, AND GALBRAITH **CONTRADICTED** THE SUPPLY-DEMAND MODEL OF PRICE. IN ALL CASES, PRICE IS SET BY **BARGAINING POWER**, AND SUPPLY AND DEMAND ARE ALWAYS GOING TO BE IMPORTANT ELEMENTS OF BARGAINING POWER.

The supply-demand model of price just **excludes** other elements of bargaining power in order to visualize the interactions between supply and demand more clearly.

DEMAND SUPPLY

What we've seen for the past few pages is how nonmainstream economists tried to add **other** elements of bargaining power to the analysis.

DEMAND SUPPLY

BUY!

This nonmainstream approach was influential in the 1960s and 1970s, but in the end it didn't catch on.

Maybe that was because nobody came up with a complete, coherent *theory* of big business. The situation reminds me of pages 19-20, when the physiocrats *lived* in a market economy but couldn't *explain* it. So they focused on the farming economy, which they *could* explain.

In a weird way, Adam Smith had to *explain* the market economy before people could really *see* it.

In the 1960s, big business had dominated parts of the economy for a century, but nobody had come up with a complete theory of it. So people focused on the *market* economy, which they *could* explain.

AS FAR AS I KNOW, NOBODY'S *EVER* EXPLAINED BIG BUSINESS FULLY. BUT THAT DOESN'T MEAN WE SHOULD IGNORE IT. IT *EXISTS*, AND IT INFLUENCES OUR ECONOMY, OUR CULTURE, AND OUR POLITICS.

NIXON

Speaking of politics, let's check out the 1968 presidential election, won by the Republican candidate, Richard Nixon, and his excellent **advertising campaign**.

NEW NIXON

NOW WITH GRAVITAS™

Sometimes President Nixon seemed like a right-winger, like when he **expanded** the Vietnam War. . . .

Sometimes Nixon seemed like a lefty, like when he finally pulled America out of the Vietnam War, reached an understanding or **détente** with the Soviets, and talked to the Communist Chinese.

THE COLD WAR'S OVER!

Heck, sometimes Nixon seemed like a full-on **socialist**: He proposed universal health care, he spent more on the poor than LBJ had, and from 1971 to 1973 he tried to stop inflation by **freezing wages and prices**.

Freezing wages and prices was extreme, but inflation was eroding the system we saw on page 134. By the early 1970s, the dollar had lost so much value that gold was flowing out of American vaults (Americans still couldn't own gold, but foreigners **could**).

GIMME AN OUNCE OF GOLD FOR 35 OF YOUR INFLATED DOLLARS.

UM, YOU'RE NOT SUPPOSED TO REALLY **DO** THAT—

GOLD WINDOW

I SAID GIMME.

In 1971, Nixon did the only thing he could: He took the dollar off the gold standard.

GOLD WINDOW

CLOSED

By 1973, the entire Bretton Woods system of fixed exchange rates had broken down. That was also the year inflation **really** took off, thanks to the **energy crisis**.

To understand the energy crisis, it's worth reminding ourselves just how much work was being done by **machines** by the 1970s.

NOT TOO LONG AGO, OUR ANCESTORS WERE LUCKY IF THEY HAD A *SINGLE* HORSE TO HELP WITH THE WORK. BY THE 1970S, MOST AMERICANS HAD THE EQUIVALENT OF *HUNDREDS* OF HORSES WORKING FOR THEM.

THESE MACHINES MOSTLY RAN OFF *FOSSIL FUEL*, INCREASINGLY *OIL*.

By the 1970s, U.S. oil production had peaked.

MONTHLY U.S. OIL PRODUCTION

THOUSANDS

350
300
250
200
150
100
50
0

1920 1930 1940 1950 1960 1970 1980 1990 2000

Overseas, the big, obvious oil fields had already been discovered and claimed. At first they were run by Western oil companies, with minimal payments to the locals.

HERE'S THIS YEAR'S ROYALTIES.

Eventually the locals won more control; in 1960, they formed the Organization of the Petroleum Exporting Countries (OPEC).

Many OPEC nations were Arab; when the U.S. took Israel's side in the October War of 1973, OPEC cut off the oil.

The price of oil shot up, and so did the cost of things made or transported using oil, which was *everything*. This was *supply-push inflation*, when rising costs of supplies increase prices all down the line.

For instance, with mechanized agriculture, expensive oil meant expensive *food*.

For most Americans that was an inconvenience; elsewhere it was a disaster.

WHERE'S THE FOOD?

THE RETURN OF MALTHUS

In Africa, 17 countries had famines in 1974.

One reason was **political**; these countries weren't democracies. No true democracy has ever had mass starvation (as of 2011).

IF WE HAD POLITICAL POWER, WE'D USE IT TO MAKE SURE WE GOT FED!

Another problem: Some Western aid helped **Western producers** more than the recipients.

HERE'S MONEY FOR A NEW DAM, AND A LIST OF OUR COMPANIES WHO WILL BUILD IT FOR YOU!

SO YOU'RE BASICALLY GIVING MONEY TO YOUR OWN COMPANIES.

YES, BUT YOU GET A DAM OUT OF THE DEAL!

BUT WE NEED WELLS MORE THAN DAMS. A DAM WILL FLOOD SOME OF OUR BEST FARMLAND.

Even good news could create problems. For instance, as the Third World got the benefits of Western medicine and sanitation, death rates **dropped**.

NO PROBLEM! WE'LL SEND YOU FOOD AID!

BUT THAT'S JUST GIVING MONEY TO YOUR OWN FARMERS. AND WHAT IF THE AID STOPS?

HEY, ARE YOU **TURNING DOWN** A DAM?

MOST OF MY SIBLINGS DIED, BUT ALL OF MY CHILDREN *LIVED*!

...NO.

Which meant **population** climbed.

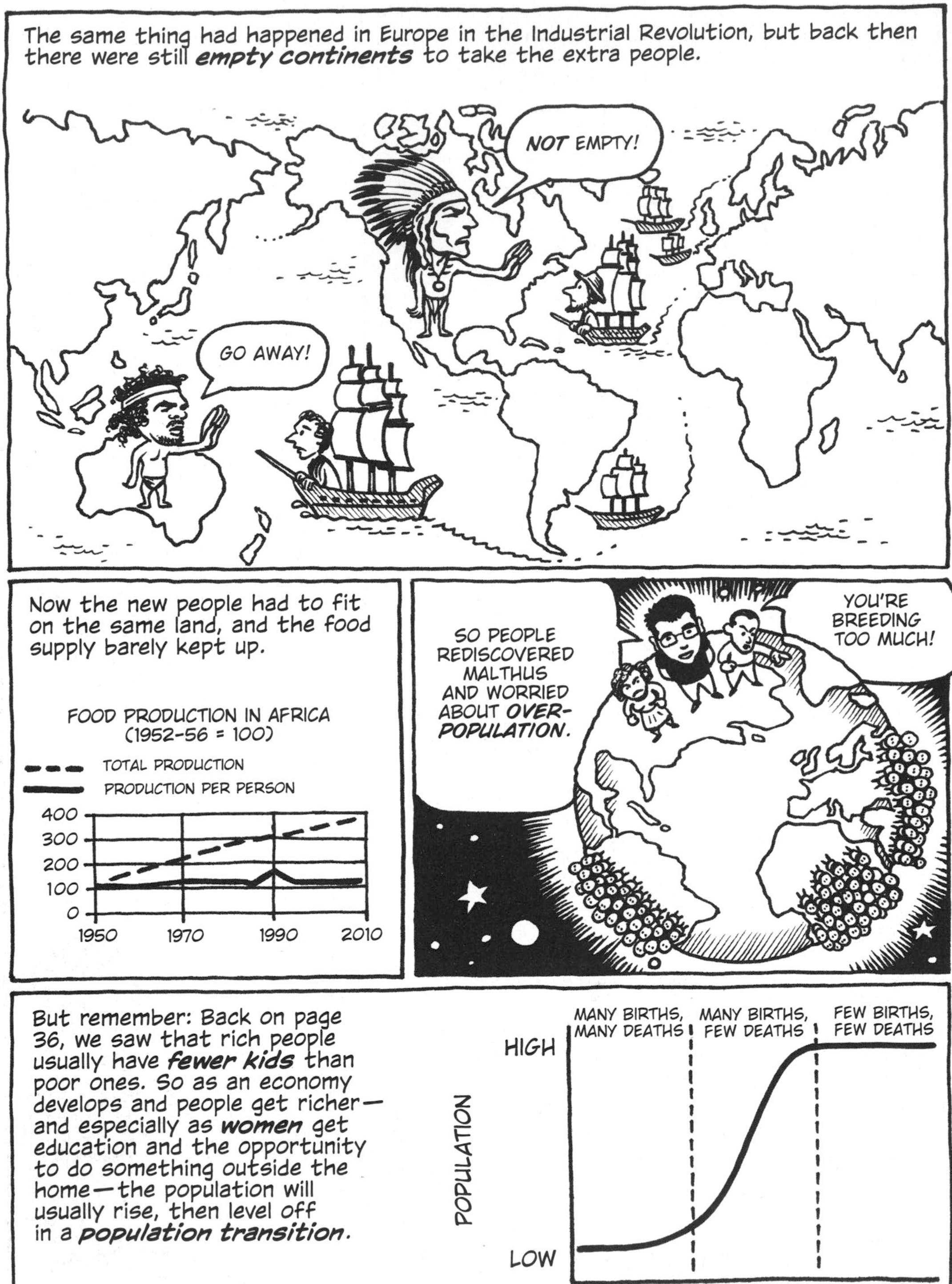

The same thing had happened in Europe in the Industrial Revolution, but back then there were still **empty continents** to take the extra people.

NOT EMPTY!

GO AWAY!

Now the new people had to fit on the same land, and the food supply barely kept up.

FOOD PRODUCTION IN AFRICA
(1952-56 = 100)

--- TOTAL PRODUCTION
— PRODUCTION PER PERSON

400
300
200
100
0

1950   1970   1990   2010

SO PEOPLE REDISCOVERED MALTHUS AND WORRIED ABOUT **OVER-POPULATION.**

YOU'RE BREEDING TOO MUCH!

But remember: Back on page 36, we saw that rich people usually have **fewer kids** than poor ones. So as an economy develops and people get richer— and especially as **women** get education and the opportunity to do something outside the home—the population will usually rise, then level off in a **population transition**.

MANY BIRTHS, MANY DEATHS   MANY BIRTHS, FEW DEATHS   FEW BIRTHS, FEW DEATHS

HIGH

POPULATION

LOW

TIME

But waiting for everyone to get rich has its own problems. Here's the catch: Although most econ texts see the economy like **this** . . .

TAXES

TAXES

GOVERNMENT

$

$

SPENDING

HOUSEHOLDS

BUSINESSES

PURCHASES

PRODUCTS

WORK

WAGES

$

$

BANKS

SAVINGS

INVESTMENT

that view leaves out something important.

RESOURCES

WASTE

We rely on **nature** to turn waste back into resources.

RESOURCES

CROPS

WOOD

AIR

CLEAN WATER

FERTILE SOIL

POOP

CO²

SMOG

WASTE-WATER

DEAD SOIL

WASTE

But nature can handle only so much. If it's **overloaded**, resources disappear and wastes build up.

RICH PEOPLE CONSUME AND WASTE MORE THAN POOR PEOPLE DO, WHICH PUTS "OVERPOPULATION" IN A DIFFERENT LIGHT.

Ecological footprint— amount of the earth's surface needed to provide a person's resources and absorb his or her waste

WE'RE NOT THE PROBLEM!

BY THE 1970S, PEOPLE WERE WARNING THAT WE WERE APPROACHING **LIMITS TO GROWTH**, BOTH POPULATION **AND** ECONOMIC GROWTH.

It's also true that more people mean more **brains**—brains that can solve problems.

OLD WHEAT

food

Not food

NEW WHEAT

food

Not food

For instance, the food crisis of the 1970s passed thanks in part to the brain of the agronomist Norman Borlaug, who developed new **green revolution** crops that multiplied food production in a non-Malthusian manner.

U.S. farm policy also changed in the early 1970s; instead of working to keep farm prices stable, which had sometimes meant paying farmers not to grow, the government started pushing for **maximum production**.

MORE! MORE! MORE!

The new policies favored big producers, or **agribusiness**, spelling the doom of the old family farm.

"Get big or get out." —Earl Butz, secretary of agriculture (1971-1976)

Agribusinesses were too big to pay attention to every acre; it was easier to plant **one thing everywhere** and call it a day. That one thing was often **corn**.

Soon the U.S. had more corn than it knew what to do with, so **new uses** for corn were found:

Corn was fed to cows. A corn diet made cows **sick**, so they needed drugs **all the time**—drugs that entered our food and water supplies and helped breed drug-resistant **superbugs**.

Corn was fed to **humans** in new forms, like **high-fructose corn syrup**,* which contributed to the rise of **obesity** in the U.S.

Corn was turned into **ethanol**, a heavily subsidized renewable fuel that makes no sense except as a giveaway to agribusiness.

WE GROW CORN TO MAKE FUEL, AND WE USE FUEL TO GROW CORN!

HOW MUCH FUEL IS LEFT OVER WHEN YOU'RE DONE?

BIG SWILL

LEFT OVER?

*Possibly because it was worse for humans than other sugars, and certainly because subsidies made it so cheap that food producers put it in everything.

But we're getting ahead of ourselves; back in the 1970s, cheap food was a blessing to Americans, many of whom had **less money** than they once did.

THE GREAT TAX INCREASE

In the 1970s, people had less money *even if their pay kept up with inflation*, thanks to *bracket creep*.

THE BRACKET CREEP STOLE OUR MONEY!

GET HIM!

NERK NERK!

Bracket creep is a misleading phrase; really, tax brackets *didn't* creep up with inflation.

VERY HIGH TAX

HIGH TAX

MEDIUM TAX

LOW TAX

So incomes that kept up with inflation crept into higher and higher tax brackets.

BUT MY PAY DOESN'T *BUY* ANY MORE!

VERY HIGH

HIGH

MEDIUM

LOW

That contributed to a major *tax increase*.

FEDERAL TAXES TAKEN OUT OF THE PAYCHECKS OF THE MEDIAN FAMILY

PERCENT OF INCOME

25
20
15
10
5
0

12

20

1965

1975

The median family is the family smack in the middle, with half of families making more and half making less.

The government didn't fix bracket creep because it *needed* to take more from ordinary people; it was taking *less* from rich people and big businesses.

Rich people and big businesses paid less every year because the tax code became more **complicated** every year, with more **loopholes**.

OK, YOU OWE, UM... HOLD ON...

I DON'T OWE ANYTHING!

REALLY? HUH.

Fixing the tax code, dealing with inflation, improving employment, cutting dependence on foreign oil—all of these problems needed vision and ideas, which weren't forthcoming from President Nixon; Nixon was paralyzed by the Watergate scandal and resigned in 1974.

Nixon's successor, Gerald Ford, had ideas, but they were just embarrassing.

LET'S ALL WEAR "WHIP INFLATION NOW" BUTTONS!

ALAN G.   WIN   WIN   WIN

Mainstream economists weren't much help.

The nonmainstream economics we saw on pages 167-173 was still influential, but it was losing ground to **another type** of nonmainstream economics, a revived defense of **laissez-faire**. Let's check that out.

THE PROPHETS OF LIBERTY: Hayek and Friedman

Way back in the 1920s, the Austrian economists Ludwig von Mises (1881–1973) and Friedrich Hayek (1899–1992) saw *economic planning* become *political dictatorship* in country after country. They saw that when people lose their *economic* liberty, they lose their *political* liberty.

WHY NOT TURN THINGS BACK TO THE *FREE MARKET*?

MISES

HAYEK

PLANNING ISN'T REALLY WORKING OUT SO HOT.

These ideas are called *neoliberalism* because they revived 19th-century liberalism, which thought that government should be too small to oppress people.

Hayek especially was a formidable thinker; instead of *assuming* the market worked, which economists had been doing since Ricardo, Hayek looked at *how* it worked— how the interaction of small units (people) creates a complex *intelligence* (the market), which responds to shortages, changes in taste, or new technologies far better than any human planner can. ("Invisible *brain*" might be a better term than "invisible *hand.*")

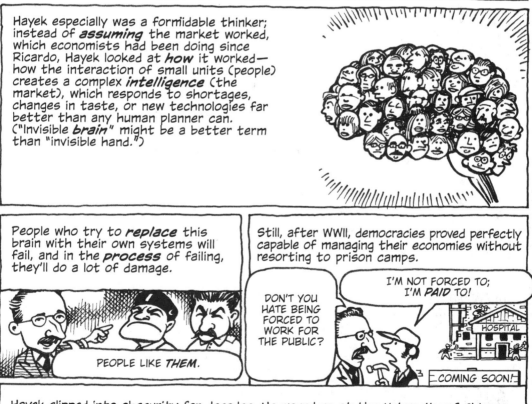

People who try to *replace* this brain with their own systems will fail, and in the *process* of failing, they'll do a lot of damage.

PEOPLE LIKE *THEM.*

Still, after WWII, democracies proved perfectly capable of managing their economies without resorting to prison camps.

DON'T YOU HATE BEING FORCED TO WORK FOR THE PUBLIC?

I'M NOT FORCED TO; I'M *PAID* TO!

HOSPITAL

COMING SOON!

Hayek slipped into obscurity for decades. He wound up at the University of Chicago, where the neoliberal mantle was picked up by the American economist *Milton Friedman* (1912–2006).

Friedman's ideas were basically an extreme defense of laissez-faire...

PEOPLE ARE MOTIVATED BY SELF-INTEREST.

IF WE LEAVE PEOPLE **FREE TO CHOOSE** THE TRANSACTIONS THAT PROMISE THEM THE BEST ADVANTAGE, THEY'LL MAXIMIZE THEIR OWN WELFARE.

THE FREE MARKET REWARDS PEOPLE FOR CONTRIBUTING TO OTHERS' WELFARE.

SO WHEN GOVERNMENT DOESN'T INTERFERE, PEOPLE MAXIMIZE THEIR OWN SELF-INTEREST BY HELPING OTHERS.

CAPITALISM AND FREEDOM

FREE TO CHOOSE

WHENEVER POSSIBLE, GOVERNMENT SHOULD BUTT OUT!

with one nod to John Maynard Keynes: Government *did* have to manage over-all demand. But instead of doing that by Keynesian adjustments of taxing and spending, Friedman recommended *increasing the money supply* by 3% or so every year (*monetarism*).

SIMPLE!

Like Hayek, Friedman stressed that **concentrated power** is a **threat** to **freedom**. But he didn't seem to see that power can concentrate in more than one form.

INSTEAD, HE COMPARED REAL-WORLD GOVERNMENTS WITH A **MODEL FREE MARKET**. AND OF COURSE TEXTBOOK MODELS WORK BETTER THAN REAL-WORLD INSTITUTIONS —THAT'S WHY WE DREAM THEM UP IN THE FIRST PLACE. FOR INSTANCE, MONETARISM WORKS **ONLY** IN NARROW ECONOMIC MODELS; IT HAS FAILED OVER AND OVER IN THE REAL WORLD.

And really, by the time Friedman started becoming prominent in the 1960s, it was clear that laissez-faire didn't necessarily work even in theory. Let's check out **market failure**.

MARKET FAILURE DOESN'T REFER TO HOW MARKETS TAKE CARE OF THE WHIMS OF THE RICH BEFORE THE NEEDS OF THE POOR. THAT'S THE MARKET **WORKING.**

Or how markets, left to themselves, often wind up **controlled.**

LEMONADE

RATHER, IT REFERS TO HOW EVEN TEXTBOOK-PERFECT MARKETS CAN GIVE BAD RESULTS—FOR INSTANCE, WITH **EXTERNALITIES,** WHICH ARE ESSENTIALLY **SIDE EFFECTS** OF ECONOMIC TRANSACTIONS.

CAVIAR

Bad externalities are everywhere, because the people making the decisions aren't the ones getting hurt.

BETTER OFF

WIDGETS INC.

HOW WAS I "FREE TO CHOOSE"?

WORSE OFF

Externalities can also be **good.** If you build a beautiful building instead of a merely functional one, everyone benefits.

But since you pay the **full** cost, while you get only **part** of the benefit, you're not motivated enough to do it.

SO A FREE MARKET, **EVEN IN THEORY,** WILL GIVE US TOO FEW *GOODS* WITH WIDELY SHARED BENEFITS AND TOO MANY WITH WIDELY SHARED COSTS.

PRIVATE AFFLUENCE AND PUBLIC SQUALOR!

Now remember page 23? Free markets work properly only when the **price** of a product reflects the **cost** to society.

Widget bill of sale $2

So if government **corrects** an externality—by taxing pollution, say—the market runs **better**.

Bill $2
+ cleaning up mine tailings $1
+ restoring polluted air and water $1.50
+ restocking dead fish $ .50
= $5.00

The big objection:

THAT WOULD MAKE MY GOODS **TOO EXPENSIVE!** YOU'LL DRIVE ME OUT OF BUSINESS!

WHICH IS **EXACTLY THE POINT**: IF WE DON'T WANT SOMETHING ENOUGH TO PAY THE **FULL** COST OF BRINGING IT TO MARKET, THEN IT'S A **BAD USE OF SOCIETY'S RESOURCES.**

ANYWAY, CORRECTING EXTERNALITIES IS OFTEN CHEAP. **THESE** WERE ALL SAID TO BE RUINOUSLY EXPENSIVE UNTIL WE **DID** THEM.

Selling gasoline without lead in it

Cutting ozone-destroying chlorofluoro-carbons

Cutting sulfur emissions that cause acid rain

Providing seat belts and air bags in cars

Improving car mileage

Improving workplace safety

Etc., etc., etc.

Even in an idealized free market, there's a role for government. Friedman acknowledged this in theory. But in practice he argued against nearly everything that government did, from licensing doctors to running Social Security.

WITH SOCIAL SECURITY, THE GOVERNMENT TAXES YOU NOW AND PAYS YOU LATER.

RIGHT.

SO IT'S **FORCING** YOU TO PROVIDE FOR YOUR RETIREMENT! YOU'RE **OPPRESSED!**

I AM?

There were others more extreme than Friedman. The University of Chicago, especially, was the breeding ground of a new **conservative economics**.

GOVERNMENT SHOULD **NEVER** INTERVENE IN THE ECONOMY! LAISSEZ-FAIRE!

One reason: In the 1970s, government wasn't all that **attractive** anymore.

THE BLOATED STATE

Taxes were too high.

Trusting the government was naive.

Programs that had served their purpose never seemed to stop.

DID YOU BRING US HIGH-SPEED RAIL?

CLEAN POWER?

RENOVATED SCHOOLS?

NO! I BROUGHT *MORE HIGHWAYS!*

BLUE PRINT

"A government bureau is the nearest thing to eternal life we'll ever see on this earth." —Ronald Reagan (1911-2004)

AND REGULATION HAD PILED ON REGULATION.

RED TAPE

Consider this bizarre 1969 regulation:

VINE-RIPENED TOMATOES MUST BE AT LEAST 2 17/32 INCHES IN DIAMETER. GREEN TOMATOES MAY BE SMALLER.

You might think American tomato growers **hated** that, but in fact they'd **demanded** it. Thing is, they mainly grew green tomatoes, while Mexican producers mainly grew vine-ripened ones. The law kept out **half** the Mexican crop, letting American growers charge 30% more.

FLORIDA

MEXICO

This sort of **regulatory capture** was a growing problem with big government: It was being taken over by the very interests it was supposed to regulate.

In the 1970s, even the key justification of big government—big business is a threat that must be kept in check—seemed **wrong**.

BIG BUSINESS IS *ON THE ROPES!*

MANAGEMENT BY NUMBERS

Business's problems really started after World War II as corporations **grew** and **diversified**. Eventually top management couldn't keep track of all the specifics. But all businesses had two things in common:

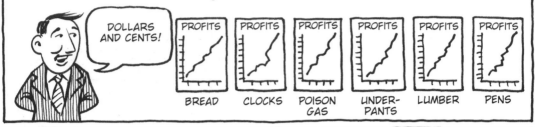

DOLLARS AND CENTS!

PROFITS — BREAD
PROFITS — CLOCKS
PROFITS — POISON GAS
PROFITS — UNDER-PANTS
PROFITS — LUMBER
PROFITS — PENS

Running these giant organizations required a new type of specialist, a specialist in **management**, who understood **money** and **numbers** instead of the details of how cars or socks got made.

PROFIT

LOSS

COST-BENEFIT ANALYSIS

RETURN ON INVESTMENT

BUSINESS SCHOOL

ETC.

These management specialists brought objective, quantitative thinking that many companies needed. But all too often, they ignored whatever **wasn't** a number, no matter how important it was.

"Every quantitative measurement we have shows us that we're winning the [Vietnam] war."
—Robert McNamara, secretary of defense under JFK and LBJ, a pioneer of this new management

For instance, when a car came off a Detroit assembly line, inspectors would check it for problems. But more and more:

FIRE THE INSPECTORS.

WHAT? WHY?

THEIR SALARIES COST MONEY, AND THEY KEEP FINDING PROBLEMS, WHICH ALSO COST MONEY.

BUT THEY KEEP OUR CARS' QUALITY HIGH.

I DON'T SEE THAT ON MY BALANCE SHEET. FIRE THEM.

Meanwhile, managers rarely noticed the cost of their **own** salaries; by the 1970s, one U.S. Steel plant had **700** managers for only 6,000 workers.

FASTER!

FASTER!

WE HAVE TO CUT COSTS!

"So much of what we call management consists of making it difficult for people to work." —Peter Drucker, management guru

With all the management, workers cared less and less...

"PROUD OF MY WORK? HOW CAN I FEEL PRIDE IN A JOB WHERE I CALL A FOREMAN'S ATTENTION TO A MISTAKE, A BAD PIECE OF EQUIPMENT, AND HE'LL IGNORE IT."
— PHIL STALLINGS, SPOT-WELDER

"THE CORPORATION COULD SET UP WAYS TO CHECK IT SO WHEN THE PRODUCT GOES TO THE CONSUMER IT SHOULD BE WHOLE, CLEAN, AND RIGHT. BUT THEY'VE LAID OFF INSPECTORS, 'CAUSE THEY COULD GIVE A $#!% LESS."
— GARY BRYNER, PRESIDENT OF A UAW LOCAL

"YOU KNOW WHAT ANOTHER PROBLEM IS TODAY? THE UPPER ECHELON OF THE MANAGEMENT HASN'T THE FAINTEST IDEA OF WHAT'S GOING ON IN THE BUSINESS."
— ANTHONY RUGGIERO, INDUSTRIAL INVESTIGATOR

"WHENEVER WE MAKE A MISTAKE, WE ALWAYS SAY, 'DON'T WORRY ABOUT IT, SOME DINGALING'LL BUY IT.'"
— JIM GRAYSON, SPOT-WELDER

All from interviews in Studs Terkel's book *Working*, 1974.

Managers even tried their hand at technical decisions. In the 1970s, designing a headlight at GM took 15 meetings, 5 of which included the **CEO**.

And when Lee Iacocca, president of Ford from 1970 to 1978, wanted a compact car, he decided the specifications, which was OK.

MAKE IT WEIGH LESS THAN 2,000 POUNDS AND COST LESS THAN $2,000.

Note that the price was **set** before the car was even designed.

Iacocca **also** decided how long it would take, which was less OK.

START TOOLING UP.

BUT THE DESIGN'S NOT DONE.

I **SAID**, START TOOLING UP.

THE RESULTING FORD PINTO TENDED TO **BURST INTO FLAMES**. THIS PROBLEM COULD HAVE BEEN FIXED FOR $11 PER CAR BUT WASN'T.

The car companies weren't unique. Bad management helped bring down the giant Penn Central Railroad and U.S. Steel in the 1970s.

THE PENN CENTRAL COLLAPSE FORCED THE GOVERNMENT TO NATIONALIZE PASSENGER RAIL. THE PUBLIC SYSTEM— AMTRAK—IS NO GEM, BUT IT DOES BETTER THAN THE PENN CENTRAL DID.

Anyway, companies had no lack of excuses.

UNIONS!

ENVIRONMENTAL LAWS!

FOREIGN COMPETITION!

THE PROBLEM IS TAXES!

MEDDLESOME REGULATIONS!

There was some truth to these excuses, especially **foreign competition**.

MADE IN JAPAN

Big U.S. companies had taken their customers for granted for decades.

THE **FORD PINTO**

IT LEAVES YOU WITH THAT WARM FEELING

Actual slogan!

Meanwhile, *international trade* kept getting more efficient.

The container ship, invented in 1956

By the 1970s, American companies accustomed to dominating a national market found themselves **competing** in a global market.

Most visibly, Americans started buying *foreign cars*, especially Japanese ones.

WHAT'S THAT?

IT'S A TOYOTA.

A TOY WHAT?

Japan's government protected its businesses from imports, encouraged them to cooperate, gave them subsidies and favors, and practically forced citizens to save so business always had investment coming in.

BUT IF OUR CONSUMERS SAVE THEIR MONEY, WHO'LL BUY OUR STUFF?

FOREIGNERS!

Americans complained that Japan's policies were unfair, which they were, but the real problem was that Japanese companies were making **better stuff** than American ones.

IT'S EASY TO CATCH UP WHEN YOUR RIVAL'S GOING BACKWARD!

Japanese companies had fewer managers, and their managers were less aloof. Even in the 2000s, Japanese car companies still got **100 times** more suggestions from their employees than American companies did.

OUR MANAGERS *LISTEN!*

Since Americans bought cars with dollars, Japan wound up with dollars. What to do with them?

A DOLLAR WON'T BUY GROCERIES IN TOKYO!

Dollars would buy American goods, but the Japanese didn't buy as much as they sold—that is, the U.S. ran a **trade deficit**.

ELECTRONICS CARS CARS ELECTRONICS
JAPAN
WHEAT MOVIES
U.S.

Dollars would also buy American **capital**—stocks, bonds, government debt, and so on. This trade had once been restricted, but the restrictions, or **capital controls**, were relaxed in the 1970s.

So the flow of **money** balanced, while the flow of **goods** didn't.

CARS CARS CARS
JAPAN
REAL ESTATE STOCKS & BONDS
U.S.

EVER SINCE, THE U.S. HAS SOLD OFF **CAPITAL** TO PAY FOR MORE STUFF.

That's been good for Americans who **own** capital.

I'LL PAY $10 MILLION FOR THAT BUILDING.

I'LL PAY $15 MILLION!

And good for American consumers.

JOHN'S CAR DEALS

NONEXPLOSIVE CARS! CHEAP!

But remember: Most consumers are also **workers**.

FORD

MOSTLY MALAISE

Jimmy Carter, the Democrat who won the presidency in 1976, had a lot to deal with.

AMERICAN MFG CORPORATION

CLOSED

BREAD
BREAD 10¢ 20¢ 35¢

UNEMPLOYMENT OFFICE

CARTER **DEREGULATED** TRUCKING, AIRLINES, TELECOMMUNICATIONS, AND FINANCE.

That worked reasonably well. In air travel, airlines were less **protected**, so upstarts could challenge them. The price of air tickets fell (mostly).

ALTHOUGH **SERVICE** WENT DOWNHILL, TOO.

MORE IMPORTANT, CARTER DEREGULATED **BEER**. IN THE 1970S, THERE WERE ONLY A FEW BIG BREWERS; THEIR BEER TASTED LIKE SOMETHING FROM A GOVERNMENT BEER AUTHORITY. CARTER ALLOWED **HOME BREWING**, WHICH LED TO TODAY'S SMALL BREWERIES AND EXCELLENT BEER.

IN FACT, WHEN **CONSERVATIVES** POINT TO SUCCESSFUL DEREGULATIONS, THEY MOSTLY POINT TO CARTER'S. LATER DEREGULATIONS DIDN'T WORK OUT SO WELL.

BANK

President Carter, though, was no apostle of laissez-faire. When Chrysler stumbled in the late 1970s, Carter gave Lee Iacocca, the new CEO, breathing space to turn things around, which he did.

Carter also tried hard to deal with the national addiction to *fossil fuels*.

Solar thermal panels, removed by President Reagan in the 1980s.

However, that wasn't enough to deal with another *oil crisis* (1979):

Oil prices shot up when religious fundamentalists seized power in Iran, took Americans hostage, and wouldn't give them back.

WHAT HAVE WE EVER DONE TO THEM?

FIGHT U.S. IMPERIALISM

What with the price of gas, the hostage humiliation, and a sharp recession, Carter lost the 1980 election to *Ronald Reagan*, former governor of California.

[Profit] is always highest in countries which
are going fastest to ruin.

—Adam Smith, *The Wealth of Nations* (1776)

CHAPTER 7

THE
REVOLT
OF THE
RICH

(1980–2001)

Before we go on, let's remind ourselves how the rich and powerful have made *their* interest seem like *everyone's* interest.

MONOPOLIES ARE GOOD!

OWNING SLAVES IS GOOD!

PUTTING EVERYONE IN PRISON CAMPS WILL CREATE A SOCIALIST PARADISE!

FACTORY REGULATIONS ARE BAD!

LETTING THE POOR DIE IS BEST FOR EVERYONE!

Adam Smith described it pretty well:

"ALL FOR OURSELVES, AND NOTHING FOR OTHER PEOPLE, SEEMS, IN EVERY AGE OF THE WORLD, TO HAVE BEEN THE VILE MAXIM OF THE MASTERS OF MANKIND."

It's easy enough to dismiss these ideas now. But in their day, they *worked*.

THEY "CONFOUNDED THE COMMON SENSE OF MANKIND"!

Similar ideas confound our common sense *today*.

POLLUTION CONTROLS ARE BAD!

HIGH TAXES ON THE RICH ARE BAD!

UNREGULATED FINANCIAL MARKETS ARE GOOD!

SOCIAL PROGRAMS ARE BAD!

These ideas really started spreading in the 1970s, when a few big-money players like Andrew Mellon's grandnephew, Richard Mellon Scaife, set up a network of institutions to advocate them, creating the core of a *conservative movement*.

THINK TANK

TV STATION

NEWSPAPER

PUBLISHER

UNIVERSITY

BOOK CLUB

SO IN THE "MARKETPLACE OF IDEAS," SOME IDEAS HAVE BEEN **HEAVILY SUBSIDIZED.**

Oh, rich folks are the state's salvation.
They engage in wealth creation.
They deserve their compensation.
Taxes sap their motivation.
Vex them not with regulation.
That's the way to save the nation!

DAILY GRIND

NOW HERE'S THE THING: I'VE BEEN TAKING **POLITICAL STANDS** ALL ALONG. BUT UP UNTIL NOW, THIS BOOK MIGHT NOT HAVE **SEEMED** ALL THAT POLITICAL, BECAUSE THE PAST IS OVER. SAYING THAT **SLAVERY IS WRONG** ISN'T VERY CONTROVERSIAL TODAY.

AT LEAST AMONG SANE PEOPLE.

BUT IF THIS BOOK HAD COME OUT IN THE 1850S, THAT POINT OF VIEW WOULD HAVE BEEN **PLENTY** CONTROVERSIAL.

I'M CONFIDENT THAT **TODAY'S** JUSTIFICATIONS FOR EXTREME INEQUALITIES OF WEALTH AND POWER ARE HORSEPUCKEY, JUST LIKE YESTERDAY'S, AND WILL FADE AWAY AS COMPLETELY.

BUT FOR NOW, MANY PEOPLE DISAGREE, WHICH MEANS THIS BOOK IS ABOUT TO GET MORE **CONTROVERSIAL**. SO BE IT.

Anyway, what are those subsidized ideas? A big one: the **conservative economics** we saw on pages 183-186. In the 1970s, it **wasn't** horsepuckey— it was **intellectually respectable.**

After all, on page 166 we saw mainstream economists get wrapped up in math that **assumed** a perfect free market from the get-go.

It was only a small jump from there to Milton Friedman, and from Friedman to...

UNSUPERVISED MARKETS ARE ALWAYS BEST!

Thus, in the 1970s, conservative economics wasn't very far from the mainstream.

But the mainstream eventually **reengaged** with the real world.

UNSUPERVISED MARKETS CAN **SCREW UP!**

Dumb layout

Not imposed by government

By the early 2000s, the mainstream had **expanded** its models to include:

- The importance of **history** and **institutions**
- The importance of **ideas** and **knowledge**
- **Monopolistic competition** (page 168)
- **Asymmetric information** (People don't have the same information.)
- The developments in **psychology** since Ricardo's day (We're not simple, rational calculating machines.)
- Our **social** impulses, such as how we'll often choose **fairness** over private gain
- Keynes
- Reams and reams of real-world **data**
- **Controlled experiments** looking at how we **actually** act, not how theory says we **should** act
- And more!

But those expanded models are not part of our story because they haven't had much **effect.** As of 2011, our economic debates are mostly still stuck in the 1970s.

UNSUPERVISED MARKETS ARE **WONDERFUL.**

I DISAGREE. UNSUPERVISED MARKETS ARE **PERFECT.**

For instance, since the 1970s we've endlessly heard that **the rich are too poor**, and even that **the poor are too rich**. (In 2002, the *Wall Street Journal* called poor people "*lucky duckies.*")

THEY GET TOO MANY HANDOUTS FROM THE GOVERNMENT!

THEY WOULD DEVELOP MORE CHARACTER IF THEIR LIVES WERE HARDER!

THEY ALWAYS PLAY THE VICTIM WHEN THEY REALLY HAVE IT GREAT!

THEY FEEL ENTITLED TO GET PAID WITHOUT WORKING!

THEY SHOULD PAY MORE TAXES!

THE COUNTRY CAN'T AFFORD TO KEEP SUPPORTING THEM IN IDLENESS!

One might wonder how the rich **get** such insight into poor people's psyches, given how little contact the two classes have. One possibility is that they're projecting their **own** faults onto **others**. Certainly things make more sense **this** way.

WE GET TOO MANY HANDOUTS FROM THE GOVERNMENT!

WE WOULD DEVELOP MORE CHARACTER IF OUR LIVES WERE HARDER!

WE ALWAYS PLAY THE VICTIM WHEN WE REALLY HAVE IT GREAT!

WE FEEL ENTITLED TO GET PAID WITHOUT WORKING!

WE SHOULD PAY MORE TAXES!

THE COUNTRY CAN'T AFFORD TO KEEP SUPPORTING US IN IDLENESS!

ANYWAY, OTHER CONSERVATIVE IDEAS, SUCH AS GETTING RID OF TRIED-AND-TRUE MEASURES LIKE SOCIAL SECURITY, THE PROGRESSIVE TAX SYSTEM, AND SO ON, WERE ACTUALLY NOT CONSERVATIVE AT ALL—THEY WERE RATHER *RADICAL.*

In fact, conservatives of the 1970s called their movement a **revolution**, and it was. It aimed to erase the New Deal and turn the clock back to the 1920s, which brings us back to **Ronald Reagan**.

Portrait of Calvin Coolidge, which replaced a portrait of Thomas Jefferson when Reagan took office

REAGANOMICS

President Reagan promised smaller government, balanced budgets, less regulation, and **tax cuts**.

"GOVERNMENT IS NOT THE SOLUTION TO OUR PROBLEMS, GOVERNMENT IS THE PROBLEM!"

YAAAY!

People were **right** to want tax cuts; by 1980, the median family was losing 25% of its income to federal taxes. Fifteen years before, it had been **half** that.

WITH OTHER TAXES, WE'RE PAYING A **THIRD** OF OUR INCOME.

THAT'S STILL LESS THAN MOST PEOPLE PAY IN WESTERN EUROPE.

BUT WESTERN EUROPEANS **GET** MORE: FREE HEALTH CARE, GOOD SCHOOLS, CHEAP COLLEGE EDUCATIONS....

Reagan delivered. The top tax rate fell from 70% to 50% in 1981, then to a mere 28.6% in 1986. The 1986 law closed some loopholes, but opened others.

"In the case of a partnership with a taxable year beginning May 1, 1986, if such partnership realized net capital gain during the period beginning the first day of such taxable year ending on May 29, 1986, pursuant to an indemnity agreement dated May 6, 1986, then such partnership may elect to treat each asset to which such net capital gain relates as having been distributed to the partners of such partnership in proportion to their distributive share of the capital gain or loss realized by the partnership with respect to each asset."

A part of the 1986 tax law that saved the partners of Bear Stearns, a big Wall Street firm, $8 million in taxes (if applied **only** to them).

Big corporations got sweet tax cuts and Mellon-style rebates, like $150 million for GE in 1981.

Bracket creep was finally stopped—today, tax brackets move up with inflation—but regular folks only got a tax break of 1% or so. In other words, the tax increase of the 1970s was **locked in**.

HE'S NOT TAKING **MORE**, BUT WHY SHOULD HE KEEP WHAT HE HAS?

NERK NERK!

Would lower taxes mean less revenue? Reagan said *no*.

"THESE POLICIES WILL MAKE OUR ECONOMY STRONGER, AND THE STRONGER ECONOMY WILL BALANCE THE BUDGET, WHICH WE'RE COMMITTED TO DO BY 1984."

Reagan also cut some social spending, but he pumped up the military budget to the point that total spending went way up. In other words:

REAGAN MADE GOVERNMENT BIGGER

Lower taxes and more spending meant huge *budget deficits*, although Reagan may not have *understood* that: His economic policy was remarkably *casual*.

FEDERAL BUDGET, 1980-1986

BILLIONS OF $

1000 · 800 · 600 · 400 · 200 · 0

SPENDING

REVENUE

BORROWING

1980 · 1982 · 1984 · 1986

"[Reagan] doesn't acknowledge our deficits. He can't understand why people keep talking about his position on the deficit. He's been against deficits for forty years. Why should anyone question that?" —David Stockman, Reagan's first budget director

So Reagan's economic policy came down to *deficit spending*.

On page 124, we saw how deficit spending causes *booms*. But this time, not so much.

REAL GDP (IN CONSTANT 2000 DOLLARS)

TRILLIONS OF $

5.5 · 5 · 4.5 · 4

1975 1976 1977 1978 1979 1980 1981 1982 1983

After all, the tax breaks went almost exclusively to the *rich*.

Much of Reagan's spending simply **disappeared** (more than 130 members of his administration were investigated, indicted, or convicted, a new record).

UNITED STATES TREASURY

Plus, in 1982 and 1983 Reagan *raised taxes*, to the point that most people, except the rich, wound up paying more taxes than they had under Carter (although Reagan's budgets never came close to balancing).

THAT'S WORTH REPEATING, BECAUSE THE MYTH IS SO DIFFERENT:

REAGAN RAISED TAXES

The **big** reason Reagan's deficit spending didn't cause much of a boom lies in the mysterious halls of the *Federal Reserve*.

THE FED

As we saw back on page 91, the Federal Reserve keeps a handle on the money supply. In other words, it controls **monetary policy**.

The Fed can create a bank account with money in it from nothing; that's where dollars come from.

To get that money into circulation, the Fed **buys** something in an **open market** operation. The Fed usually buys government bonds.

THE FED

BANK

To take money **out** of circulation, the fed **sells** something back.

THE FED

I.O.U.

$

BANK

The Fed adds or removes money until the **funds rate**—the interest rate banks charge one another for overnight loans, which is very sensitive to changes in the money supply—moves to whatever level the Fed wants.

FUNDS   RATE

Less often, the Fed changes the **discount rate**, the interest rate banks pay to borrow directly from the Fed.

HIGH INTEREST RATES DISCOURAGE BORROWING, WHICH DISCOURAGES SPENDING. SO WHEN THE FED RAISES INTEREST RATES, IT'S **YANKING BACK** ON THE ECONOMY.

LOWERING RATES LETS THE ECONOMY EXPAND; THIS DOESN'T WORK AS WELL AS YANKING BACK, THE SAME WAY PULLING ON A BALLOON'S STRING MAKES IT FALL MORE RELIABLY THAN PUSHING ON THE STRING WILL MAKE IT RISE.

The trick is **timing**—pull money out to cool off booms and put it back before we get a slump.

IN THE DEPRESSION, THE FED GOT IT EXACTLY WRONG: IT FLOODED THE ECONOMY WITH MONEY IN THE 1920S AND YANKED THE MONEY BACK OUT IN THE EARLY 1930S.

THAT'S WHY CONSERVATIVES SAY THE DEPRESSION WAS *ENTIRELY* THE FAULT OF THE GOVERNMENT, WHICH IT WAS NOT.

From the 1940s to the 1960s, the Fed mainly got things right. But in the stagflation of the 1970s, the best course wasn't clear, and the Fed came under pressure from both sides.

INFLATION'S HIGH! RAISE INTEREST RATES!

UNEMPLOYMENT'S HIGH! LOWER INTEREST RATES!

The Fed is *independent*; it doesn't actually have to listen to anyone. When inflation hit 13% in 1979, Paul Volcker, the new chairman of the Federal Reserve, struck out on his own.

IT'S TIME TO *END* INFLATION.

Volcker raised interest rates, causing a recession in 1980, an election year.

Then came Reagan's deficit spending, which could have been very inflationary.

WHAT ARE YOU *DOING*?

To counteract Reagan's flood of money, Volcker raised interest to unheard-of levels, triggering *another* recession.

That finally brought down inflation, to the point that people stopped *expecting* prices to rise. So while people say Reagan ended the inflation of the 1970s, the credit really goes to Volcker.

HABITAT

OR TO ME, THE GUY WHO *APPOINTED* VOLCKER.

Of course, everyone had always known that a bad-enough slump would end inflation.

IF PEOPLE HAVE NO MONEY, THEY CAN'T PAY HIGHER PRICES!

THE QUESTION WAS WHETHER IT WAS *WORTH* IT. AFTER ALL, INFLATION IS ANNOYING, BUT UNEMPLOYMENT *KILLS*. ONE 1976 CONGRESSIONAL STUDY ESTIMATED THAT EACH 1% RISE IN UNEMPLOYMENT MEANT:

495 more deaths from liver cirrhosis

628 more homicides

920 more suicides

3,440 more inmates in state prisons

4,227 more admissions to mental hospitals

20,240 more fatal heart attacks and strokes

207

Anyway, when Reagan **raised taxes** in 1983, Volcker let interest rates fall; 1984 was a genuinely good year, and also an election year.

The government still ran deficits, so the Fed got into the habit of pulling back at the first **hint** of inflation, or even of rising employment; 6.5% **unemployment** was redefined as "full employment" in the Reagan years.

Add up the effects of Reagan's deficit spending and the Fed's monetary tightness and we have the basics of the **Reagan economy**.

1. The government spent lots on the military, as well as on other favors and subsidies for big business.

2. The rich, and the corporations they owned, paid low taxes.

3. The government had to borrow the money it hadn't raised from taxes . . .

4. and pay interest.

5. All the borrowing made the Fed nervous about inflation, so it kept interest rates artificially high, so the government paid **more** interest.

6. Meanwhile, ordinary people paid high 1970s taxes, plus some extra.

7. The government "couldn't afford" to spend much on them . . .

8. while high interest rates kept unemployment high and wages low.

9. People saved less and borrowed more . . .

10. and paid artificially high interest on car loans, mortgages, business loans, school loans, and credit card debt.

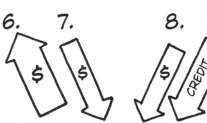

One consequence of all that: an ever-growing *national debt*—debt taken out in taxpayers' names—that nobody knew (or knows) what to do with.

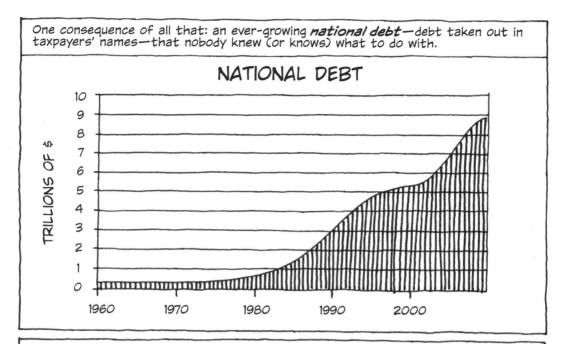

NATIONAL DEBT

Another consequence: an ever-growing pile of money in the hands of the rich, probably *more* than could be productively invested.

I say "probably" because it's not clear how much investors even tried to *find* productive investment. In the 1980s, *speculators* went wild. *Wall Street* boomed like it hadn't since the 1920s.

THE RETURN OF THE MONEY POWER

One thing to speculate in: **junk bonds**, which were IOUs offered by fly-by-night companies that were unlikely to pay back, hence "junk." **High risk** had always kept sober investors away from junk bonds, but this high risk came with **high interest.** Speculators have trouble resisting high interest; the junk market exploded in the 1980s.

WE CAN'T UNDERSTAND WHAT CAME NEXT WITHOUT REPEATING THAT **STOCKS** REPRESENT **OWNERSHIP** OF COMPANIES. WHEN YOU BUY A STOCK, YOU BECOME PART OWNER OF A COMPANY; BUY ENOUGH STOCK AND YOU **CONTROL** THE COMPANY.

For decades managers of big companies hadn't worried about anyone doing that.

WHO HAS THAT KIND OF MONEY?

But in the 1980s:

I CAN BORROW THE MONEY!

WALL STREET

JUNK BOND

Corporate raiders would sell junk bonds, use the money to take over a company, and then sell the company's assets for enough money to pay back the bonds—which suddenly didn't seem so junky after all—and leave a nice profit for themselves.

ISN'T THAT OUR PENSION FUND?

NOT ANYMORE!

One example: In the early 1980s, Gulf Oil was selling for $40 a share; at that price, the total amount of Gulf shares (the **market capitalization**) would have cost $6.5 billion. But the oil fields Gulf owned were worth **more** than that.

In 1983, the corporate raider T. Boone Pickens started buying Gulf shares. Gulf's managers didn't like Pickens; they turned to Chevron, which engulfed Gulf for $80 a share. That high price meant Pickens and his friends sold their stock for a $760 million profit, while Gulf disappeared.

"AT $40 THE COMPANY'S WORTH $6.5 BILLION, AT $80 IT'S WORTH $13 BILLION. SO EVERYBODY CAN SEE WHAT WAS CREATED THERE." —PICKENS

In real life, it's hard to see what was created except paper value. In fact, something had been *destroyed*.

"I THOUGHT I WAS WORKING FOR A GREAT SOCIAL INSTITUTION. I DIDN'T THINK I WAS GIVING AWAY 25 YEARS OF MY LIFE, WITH ALL THE COSTS FOR MY FAMILY, FOR SOME PIECES OF PAPER."

Gulf exec, after Gulf disappeared

IN OTHER WORDS, INSTEAD OF TURNING PAPER SAVINGS INTO JOBS AND INVESTMENT, THE FINANCIAL WORLD WAS DOING THE *OPPOSITE*, TURNING JOBS AND INVESTMENT INTO PAPER WEALTH.

To keep raiders away, managers had to make their companies *expensive*.

IF WE DON'T BOOST OUR STOCK PRICE, WE'LL BE TAKEN OVER AND FIRED.

At the same time, *pension funds* and *mutual funds* were concentrating the power of many individual investors on Wall Street, which then *used* that power.

WALL STREET

I MANAGE THE INVESTMENTS OF PEOPLE WHO OWN 51% OF YOUR PUNY COMPANY, AND I THINK . . .

A frantic scramble for *shareholder value* (stock price) ensued.

WALL STREET

211

According to Wall Street (and some economists), this focus on stock price was *efficient*.

WHEN I INDULGE MY GREED BY DEMANDING HIGHER STOCK PRICES, I'M FORCING COMPANIES TO **RUN BETTER.** GREED IS GOOD!

Which might have been true in the 1960s, when the typical investor held a stock for five years. But by the 1980s, stocks were bought and sold so fast that **computers** were doing more and more of the actual trading.

BUYSELL BUYBUY SELLBUY SELLSELL BUY

Wall Street focused increasingly on the **short term.**

"WELL RUN"   "POORLY RUN"

COMPANY A   COMPANY B

PROFIT

LONG-TERM INVESTMENT
RESEARCH AND DEVELOPMENT
CUSTOMER LOYALTY
WORKERS
COMMUNITY

And pleasing Wall Street meant:

"POORLY RUN"

A   COMPANY B

PROFIT

LONG-TERM INVESTMENT
ARCH AND DEVELOPMENT
CUSTOMER LOYALTY
WORKERS
COMMUNITY

Other things seemed to please Wall Street whether or not they even increased profit. **Mergers**, for one. **Layoffs**, for another.

SORRY! THE COMPANY CAN'T AFFORD YOUR SALARIES!

BUT WE'RE MAKING A PROFIT!

AND WHAT ABOUT YOUR SALARY?

AND YOUR GIGANTIC BONUS?

AND YOUR "BUSINESS TRIPS" TO THE RIVIERA ON THE CORPORATE JET?

That's another case in which the financial world should have been doing this...

PAPER WEALTH

COMPANY

REAL INVESTMENT

but did this instead:

PAPER WEALTH

CLOSED

REAL INVESTMENT

IT'S WORTH POINTING OUT HOW LITTLE THIS COMPETITION FOR STOCK PRICE RESEMBLES THE FREE-MARKET COMPETITION WE SAW ON PAGE 23.

Increasingly, big businesses didn't compete to provide a good product at a good price; they competed to extract short-term profit to win Wall Street's favor.

WE DON'T COMPETE TO PLEASE YOU.

WE COMPETE TO **SQUEEZE** YOU.

One way to make big profits: Have the government give you money.

$643.⁰⁰

$2,043.⁰⁰

Actual prices paid by the Pentagon to defense contractors in the Reagan years

CONSIDER REAGAN'S STAR WARS MISSILE DEFENSE SYSTEM. AS OF 2011, AFTER MORE THAN TWO DECADES AND $100 BILLION, IT STILL CAN'T STOP A SINGLE MISSILE (NOT THAT ANYONE WOULD SEND A **SINGLE** MISSILE ANYWAY). IT DOESN'T MAKE SENSE EXCEPT AS A TRANSFER OF MONEY FROM TAXPAYERS TO DEFENSE CONTRACTORS.

TOMATO JUICE

CHICKEN WIRE

State and local governments weren't spared. Companies that had been part of their community for generations—that in some cases had **created** their communities—started to leave when they were offered better deals elsewhere.

BRING YOUR JOBS HERE! $15 MILLION IN TAX BREAKS AND SUBSIDIES!

$30 MILLION!

$300 MILLION!

Offered by Alabama for 1,500 jobs ($200,000 per job)

TODAY, MANY BIG CORPORATIONS' PROFITS COME **ENTIRELY** FROM TAXPAYERS. **PRIVATIZED PROFITS AND SOCIALIZED LOSSES**, IT'S CALLED.

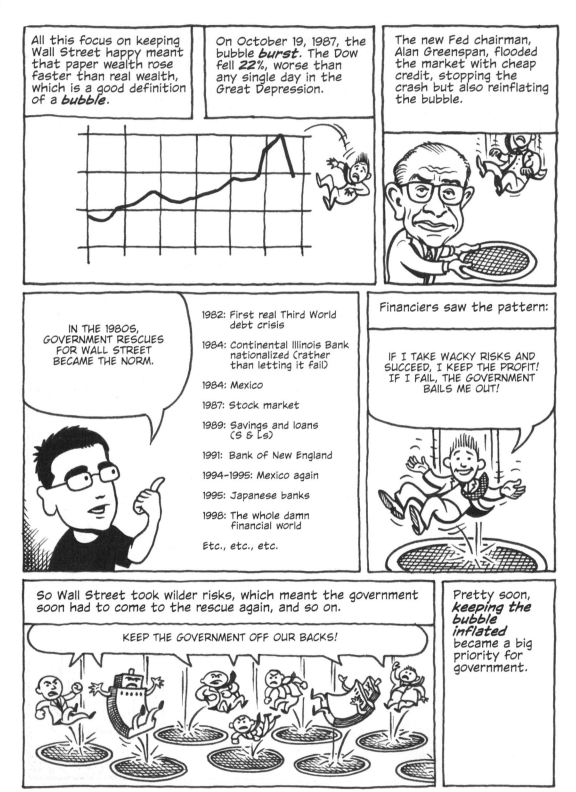

All this focus on keeping Wall Street happy meant that paper wealth rose faster than real wealth, which is a good definition of a **bubble**.

On October 19, 1987, the bubble **burst**. The Dow fell **22%**, worse than any single day in the Great Depression.

The new Fed chairman, Alan Greenspan, flooded the market with cheap credit, stopping the crash but also reinflating the bubble.

IN THE 1980S, GOVERNMENT RESCUES FOR WALL STREET BECAME THE NORM.

1982: First real Third World debt crisis

1984: Continental Illinois Bank nationalized (rather than letting it fail)

1984: Mexico

1987: Stock market

1989: Savings and loans (S & Ls)

1991: Bank of New England

1994-1995: Mexico again

1995: Japanese banks

1998: The whole damn financial world

Etc., etc., etc.

Financiers saw the pattern:

IF I TAKE WACKY RISKS AND SUCCEED, I KEEP THE PROFIT! IF I FAIL, THE GOVERNMENT BAILS ME OUT!

So Wall Street took wilder risks, which meant the government soon had to come to the rescue again, and so on.

KEEP THE GOVERNMENT OFF OUR BACKS!

Pretty soon, **keeping the bubble inflated** became a big priority for government.

PLAYING FINANCIAL INSTRUMENTS

In that sort of system, it didn't take a rocket scientist to make money.

Buy enough stock to control a company.

Make the company **buy back** the stock at a higher price.

Make the company pay a big **dividend**.

Profit.

Let's look at **buybacks**. From 1981 to early 1996, nonfinancial corporations bought back $700 billion more stock than they issued. That money could have gone to taxes or payrolls or long-term investment.

HEY, AREN'T YOU SUPPOSED TO BE PROVIDING CAPITAL TO ME?

WALL STREET

Of course, finance isn't always that easy, or that useless. Consider **derivatives**, which are essentially bets.

Bets can help **manage risk**. A bus line worried about the price of gas can go to the derivatives market and **bet** that it will rise.

WALL STREET

If the price of gas **doesn't** rise, the bus line loses the bet.

BUT I GET CHEAP GAS, SO I'M OK!

WALL STREET

If the price rises, the payoff from the bet offsets the cost.

WALL STREET

Derivatives—especially the more complex ones—are remarkably **unregulated**.

THAT WAY THEY CAN MANAGE RISK MORE EFFECTIVELY THAN IF GOVERNMENT INTERFERES!

With few rules, much of Wall Street's time came to be spent dreaming up ever-more-sophisticated *financial instruments*, or new ways to lay your bets.

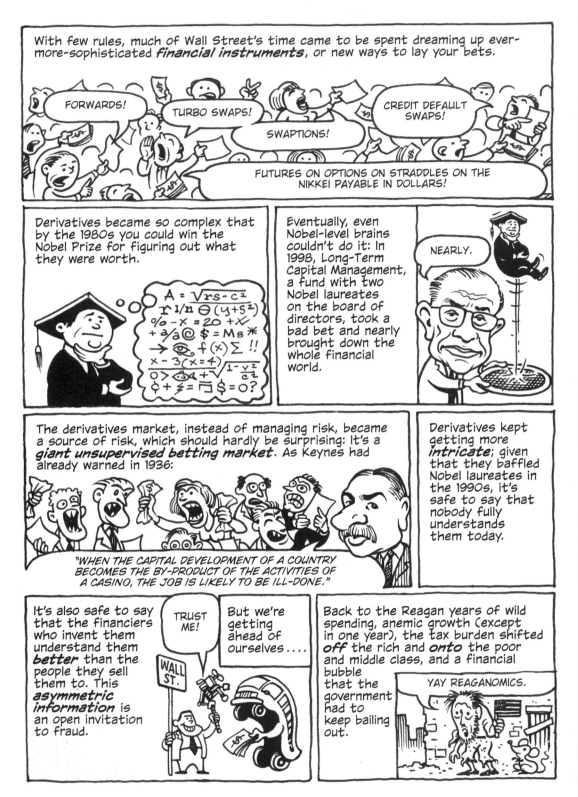

FORWARDS!

TURBO SWAPS!

SWAPTIONS!

CREDIT DEFAULT SWAPS!

FUTURES ON OPTIONS ON STRADDLES ON THE NIKKEI PAYABLE IN DOLLARS!

Derivatives became so complex that by the 1980s you could win the Nobel Prize for figuring out what they were worth.

$$A = \sqrt{rs - c^2}$$

Eventually, even Nobel-level brains couldn't do it: In 1998, Long-Term Capital Management, a fund with two Nobel laureates on the board of directors, took a bad bet and nearly brought down the whole financial world.

NEARLY.

The derivatives market, instead of managing risk, became a source of risk, which should hardly be surprising: It's a *giant unsupervised betting market*. As Keynes had already warned in 1936:

"WHEN THE CAPITAL DEVELOPMENT OF A COUNTRY BECOMES THE BY-PRODUCT OF THE ACTIVITIES OF A CASINO, THE JOB IS LIKELY TO BE ILL-DONE."

Derivatives kept getting more *intricate*; given that they baffled Nobel laureates in the 1990s, it's safe to say that nobody fully understands them today.

It's also safe to say that the financiers who invent them understand them *better* than the people they sell them to. This *asymmetric information* is an open invitation to fraud.

TRUST ME!

WALL ST.

But we're getting ahead of ourselves....

Back to the Reagan years of wild spending, anemic growth (except in one year), the tax burden shifted *off* the rich and *onto* the poor and middle class, and a financial bubble that the government had to keep bailing out.

YAY REAGANOMICS.

MORNING AFTER IN AMERICA: The Reagan Legacy

Oh, and that anemic growth wasn't *shared*.

No matter what statistics you look at, *only* the rich got richer in the 1980s, and the richer you were, the better you did.

A RISING TIDE LIFTS ALL YACHTS!

WE'RE *STILL PAYING* FOR THOSE LAME RESULTS—FOR INSTANCE, WITH THE NATIONAL DEBT . . .

plus the *foreign* debt. When Reagan took office, the U.S. was the world's biggest creditor. Soon it was the world's biggest debtor.

BONDS STOCKS

ELECTRONICS

CARS CARS

U.S. JAPAN

Not to mention neglected infrastructure, cuts in education, and an environmental policy devoted to immediate profit.

WHAT ABOUT FUTURE GENERATIONS?

"I DON'T KNOW HOW MANY GENERATIONS WE CAN COUNT ON BEFORE THE LORD RETURNS."

James Watt, secretary of the interior (1981-1983)

In fact, one reason Reagan is so well remembered is that he was gone by the time the bills came due. So let's move on to the next administration: that of George H. W. Bush.

THE S & L MESS

ONE PROBLEM REAGAN SET UP BUT BUSH HAD TO DEAL WITH: THE MISMANAGEMENT OF **SAVINGS AND LOANS** (S & LS). UNTIL THE 1970S, S & LS WERE NEIGHBORHOOD BANKS THAT, BY LAW, LENT MONEY FOR LOCAL MORTGAGES AT REGULATED INTEREST.

S & Ls would borrow money short-term and lend it long-term.

3% 6%

That made sense because short-term loans were less risky, so the interest rate was lower. And when the short-term loans came due, the S & Ls could take out another low-interest loan to pay off the first one.

But in the inflationary 1970s, interest rates rose. S & Ls had to pay high interest for money they'd locked into low-interest mortgages.

9% 6%

President Carter deregulated S & Ls a bit, but that wasn't enough. Then Reagan deregulated them **completely**...

S & LS CAN INVEST WHEREVER THEY WANT, NOT JUST IN MORTGAGES! THE MARKET WILL PROVIDE!

well, not **quite** completely. Reagan got rid of New Deal rules that made S & Ls invest their depositors' money **soberly** (previously, S & Ls had to invest their **own** money anywhere they invested their depositors' money). Reagan didn't get rid of New Deal **deposit insurance**.

So now:

Anyone could buy an S & L (they were selling for almost nothing) and accept deposits...

take wild risks with depositors' money (and *not* their own)...

keep the reward if the risks paid off...

and let *tax-payers* pay back depositors when things went wrong.

THAT, BY THE WAY, IS AN EXAMPLE OF THE ONLY REAL PATTERN I CAN FIND IN REAGAN'S DEREGULATIONS. REGULATIONS THAT ANNOYED POWERFUL INTERESTS DISAPPEARED; ONES THAT HELPED POWERFUL INTERESTS WERE LEFT IN PLACE, OR EVEN *MULTIPLIED*. IT REALLY DOES SEEM TO HAVE BEEN THAT SIMPLE.

THE PREDICTABLE (AND PREDICTED) RESULT: S & LS COLLAPSED RIGHT AND LEFT. PAYING BACK DEPOSITORS COST TAXPAYERS AROUND *HALF A TRILLION* DOLLARS, WHICH HAD TO BE BORROWED. WE'RE STILL PAYING *INTEREST* ON THAT.

Between the S & L bailout and the interest on Reagan's debt, there was little money left over for much of anything.

I WANT TO BE CALLED THE *EDUCATION PRESIDENT*!

THAT MEANS SPENDING MONEY ON SCHOOLS.

YOU DON'T UNDERSTAND: I WANT TO BE *CALLED* THE EDUCATION PRESIDENT.

The Bush years also saw some *good* news....

THE END OF THE COLD WAR

Reagan had revived the Cold War ideology, imagining a worldwide communist conspiracy poised to pounce at any moment.

EVIL EMPIRE!

In reality, the Soviets were having trouble just holding on to what they had.

ВАЛИГО НЕДЗХ

ХАРИ УЗЦ08

KOCVP

In 1980, for instance, Poland (a Soviet puppet since the end of WWII) had a nationwide wave of strikes under a *union*, Solidarity.

SOLIDARNOŚĆ

CHECK IT OUT: WORKERS STRIKING AGAINST COMMUNISTS!

LECH

The Polish strikers demanded *worker self-management* among other things.

Self-management may sound utopian, but it's not. Yugoslavia, a communist nation that stayed out of Stalin's clutches after WWII, ran its factories that way, and by the 1980s, a Yugoslav car, the Yugo, was selling in America.

NOT BAD FOR A SMALL COUNTRY THAT WAS MAINLY DEVASTATED FARMS IN 1945!

TRUE, THE YUGO WAS THE *WORST* CAR SOLD IN AMERICA, BUT THE POINT IS THAT IT WAS GOOD ENOUGH TO SELL AT ALL, LONG BEFORE, SAY, SOUTH KOREA EXPORTED CARS.

Self-management can work in capitalist economies, too—for instance, when the *employees* are also the *stockholders*.

SIMPLE!

Really, I think self-management is unwelcome because it threatens the existing **power structure**. Which is why the Soviets weren't about to try it.

Still, the Soviet **crackdown** on Solidarity in 1981 lacked the usual oomph...

WE WENT TO JAIL, BUT WE LIVED!

which was a sign that the Soviets and their puppets were **drifting**; a top-down economy needs a clear **direction**, and the Soviets no longer had one.

WE INDUSTRIALIZED IN A DECADE....

REBUILT OUR COUNTRY....

NOW WHAT?

WE BEAT HITLER....

ACHIEVED AN OKAY STANDARD OF LIVING....

HOW ABOUT SOME **FREEDOM**?

NO... THAT'S NOT IT.

True, the Soviets kept prices low.

ISN'T THAT GOOD?

But price is a form of **rationing**. Instead of going to people who were willing to pay more, goods went to people who were willing to **wait** longer.

РЫНО

With no need to compete, there was no need to be efficient. By the late 1980s, the Soviet paper industry took **seven times** more lumber to make a sheet of paper than the Finnish paper industry did.

The only real energy came from the tiny private sector.

PRIVATE PLOTS
↓
4%

COLLECTIVE FARMS

LAND

25%
PRIVATE PLOTS

COLLECTIVE FARMS

CROP PRODUCTION

Pointing out any of these problems could still land you in jail.

Then in 1985 a reformer, Mikhail Gorbachev (1931–), took over the Soviet Union.

GLASNOST (OPENNESS) IN POLITICS! *PERESTROIKA* (RESTRUCTURING) FOR THE ECONOMY!

When Gorbachev made overtures to the West, Reagan seized the opportunity.

WHAT?

WAIT . . .

Then Eastern Europeans started removing their puppet governments. In 1989 the Berlin Wall fell.

IS BEAT

Two years later the Soviet Union just *withered away*, and Gorbachev was out of a job.

The Soviet Union's collapse left a **mess**; the successor states needed help on the scale of the Marshall Plan.

WHY ARE YOU ALL LOOKING AT ME?

"WORLD'S BIGGEST ECONOMY," REMEMBER?

One obvious source of money:

WITH THE COLD WAR OVER, WE DON'T NEED OUR GIGANTIC, EXPENSIVE MILITARY!

WE'LL GET A HUGE *PEACE DIVIDEND!*

In 1990, President Bush announced big cuts to the Pentagon budget, but the very next day Saddam Hussein, dictator of Iraq, invaded Kuwait.

OOPS.

IRAQ

KUWAIT

SAUDI ARABIA

By the time the resulting Gulf War was over, the military cuts were forgotten.

"We owe Saddam a favor. He saved us from the peace dividend." —Bush administration official

So the U.S. kept its giant military, even with no enemies worth fighting.

"I'M RUNNING OUT OF DEMONS. I'M RUNNING OUT OF VILLAINS. I'M DOWN TO CASTRO AND KIM IL SUNG."

Colin Powell, chairman of the Joint Chiefs of Staff (1989-1993)

There was no money left over for the ex-Soviet world.

HAVE THESE *ECONOMISTS* INSTEAD!

The first Gulf War also made the first President Bush popular, but that wore off as the U.S. economy stayed in the tank.

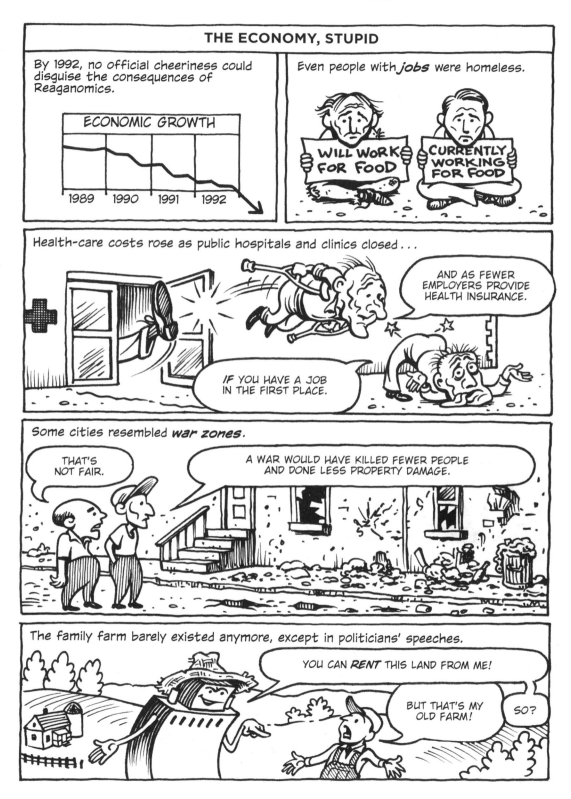

The middle class was shrinking . . .

while the upper class was **sealing itself off** in oxymoronic "gated communities."

PARANOID ACRES

No poor people

Except servants and guards

Still the burden of government **grew**.

FEDERAL SPENDING

PERCENT OF GDP

25
20.6 — 21.3
19.1 —
20

15

10

5

0

1970   1980   1990

IT'S NOT A BURDEN! GOVERNMENT IS A BURDEN WHEN IT TAXES **ME** AND SPENDS THE MONEY ON **YOU.** WHEN IT TAXES YOU AND SPENDS THE MONEY ON ME, IT'S FINE!

Bill Clinton, a Democrat, won the 1992 presidential election by tapping into a deep vein of discontent.

IT'S THE ECONOMY, STUPID!

THE PARALYZED PRESIDENT: Clinton

HEALTH CARE?

JOBS

ENVIRONMENT?

CORRUPTION?

SPRAWL

OUT

IN

IN

Before President Clinton even got started, Fed chairman Alan Greenspan and Treasury Secretary Robert Rubin explained that Wall Street came **first**.

IF YOU SPEND MONEY ON ANY OF THESE THINGS, I'LL WORRY ABOUT INFLATION, RAISE INTEREST RATES, AND SHUT DOWN THE ECONOMY.

AND BOND TRADERS WILL WORRY MORE ABOUT THE DEFICIT AND PAY LESS FOR GOVERNMENT BONDS.

SO YOU WON'T HAVE ANY MONEY TO SPEND ANYWAY.

"YOU MEAN TO TELL ME THAT THE SUCCESS OF THE ECONOMIC PROGRAM AND MY REELECTION HINGES ON THE FEDERAL RESERVE AND A BUNCH OF @^#^$% BOND TRADERS?"

YES!

IN

OUT

TOP TAX RATE

% of every extra dollar taxed in the top tax bracket

100
75
50
25
0

1960 1965 1970 1975 1980 1985 1990 1995 2000

The deficit, which was so big it worried even financiers, became priority one. Clinton's first budget **raised taxes on the rich**. The top tax rate rose to 39.6%.

Clinton's next priority:

HEALTH CARE

By the 1960s or so, every industrialized country had a universal, government-run health-care system except the U.S., which left much of its health care up to private business.

> PRIVATE BUSINESS MEANS COMPETITION, AND COMPETITION IS EFFICIENT! KEEP BUREAUCRATS OUT OF THE DOCTOR-PATIENT RELATIONSHIP!

There's nothing wrong with private doctors, but by the 1990s private *insurers* weren't competing to please customers with low premiums and good service so much as they were competing to please Wall Street with high profits.

One way to profit: Stop people who actually *need* insurance from signing up in the first place.

ACME HEALTH INSURANCE

NO SICK FOLKS

Another way: *Don't pay claims.*

DENIED
DENIED
DENIED
DENIED

Screening customers and fighting claims took *work*, which meant high *administrative costs*.

PERCENT OF PREMIUMS SPENT ON ACTUAL HEALTH CARE

85	98	99
PRIVATE	MEDICARE	CANADIAN HEALTH SYSTEM

(y-axis: 0, 20, 40, 60, 80, 100)

And that's if you *had* insurance.

HOSPITAL

DON'T YOU KNOW HEALTH CARE IS *RATIONED*? IT GOES TO THOSE WHO CAN AFFORD TO PAY!

By the 1990s, it was clear that something had to be done.

Clinton's plan, spearheaded by First Lady Hillary Rodham Clinton, was a public-private partnership that pleased nobody and died.

BUT THE PLAN GIVES YOU SO MUCH!

IT DOESN'T GIVE ME *EVERYTHING!*

HEALTH CARE

Health care got even worse, and bureaucrats—sorry, "executives"—routinely interfered in the doctor-patient relationship.

I'M SCHEDULING YOUR SURGERY FOR—

AHEM.

DENIED

I MEAN, HERE'S AN ASPIRIN. GOOD-BYE.

Which brings us to 1994, when Alan Greenspan, still chairman of the Fed, raised interest rates despite *no* evidence of inflation...

thereby helping Republicans win both houses of Congress in the 1994 election.

The new legislators were true believers in the conservative revolution.

GOVERNMENT *NEVER* WORKS! IT SHOULDN'T EXIST AT ALL!

EXCEPT WHEN IT PAYS MY SALARY! AND GIVES ME EXCELLENT HEALTH CARE!

Grover Norquist, influential conservative activist

IT'S WORTH POINTING OUT THAT FROM THE NEW DEAL TO THE 1970s, GOVERNMENT POLICIES, WHATEVER THEIR FLAWS, WERE DESIGNED TO CREATE WIDESPREAD PRIVATE WEALTH, AND THEY DID. STARTING IN THE 1980s, GOVERNMENT POLICIES WERE DESIGNED TO *CONCENTRATE* THAT WEALTH IN A FEW HANDS, AND THEY DID. IT'S NOT THAT GOVERNMENT DOESN'T WORK— IT'S THAT WE SHOULDN'T ASSUME IT'S WORKING FOR *US.*

"I DON'T WANT TO ABOLISH GOVERNMENT. I SIMPLY WANT TO REDUCE IT TO THE SIZE WHERE I CAN DRAG IT INTO THE BATHROOM AND DROWN IT IN THE BATHTUB."

With Congress and the White House at odds, government was left somewhat paralyzed. So the problems of the Reagan economy stayed in place; some even got *worse.*

THE WINNER-TAKE-ALL ECONOMY

Most of the wealth created in the Clinton years went to a small group at the top, so the **gap between rich and poor** grew.

Some inequality is OK. If we all got the same income no matter what, we might not bother to work.

And lots of modern products started as *luxuries*— they might never have been made in the first place if there weren't rich people to buy them.

Rich people buy something

Manufacturers improve it and make it cheaper

Eventually most everyone can afford it

Still, there was plenty of inequality back in the 1970s, when a typical CEO got **40 times** what a typical worker did. By 2000, that was **500 times**.

NOT TO MENTION THAT NOW OUR TAXES ARE *HIGHER* AND HIS ARE *LOWER*.

People who make money like that insist:

I *NEED* IT AS AN INCENTIVE TO DO MY BEST, AND I *DESERVE* IT BECAUSE I CREATE SO MUCH WEALTH!

Let's look at Disney CEO Michael Eisner. In 1988 he was the highest-paid executive in America; he made $40 million.

In 1998, he was #1 again, but this time he made **$575 million**. It's hard to believe that the extra money made him work harder.

WERE YOU *SLACKING OFF* IN 1988?

OF COURSE NOT!

For that matter, it's hard to believe Eisner produced more value than the **10,000 well-paid teachers** we could have hired for $575 million a year.

SO WHAT DID ALL THAT EXTRA MONEY WE GAVE CEOS *BUY* US? NOT A LOT: IT TURNS OUT THAT THERE'S NO REAL CONNECTION BETWEEN EXECUTIVES' PAY AND HOW WELL THEY DO THEIR JOBS. EXECUTIVES' PAY MEASURES HOW GOOD THEY ARE AT GETTING PAID!

It's not even clear whether that extra money made its **recipients** happier. Eisner, for instance, was top dog in 1988 and top dog in 1998, and **that's** what matters.

SORRY!

The only definite effect of the extra money: Staying on top took more **conspicuous consumption**.

BEHOLD!

Wasteful consumption **trickles down**. In the 1970s, **tycoons** owned 10,000-square-foot houses; by the 1990s, **mid-level bureaucrats** did.

BEHOLD!

"EVEN [RICH PEOPLE'S] FOLLIES AND VICES ARE FASHIONABLE, AND THE GREATER PART OF MEN ARE PROUD TO IMITATE AND RESEMBLE THEM IN THE VERY QUALITIES WHICH DISHONOR AND DEGRADE THEM."
—ADAM SMITH

People who throw away their money—like taking a private jet across the country for a few holes of golf—would be **laughable** . . .

BEHOLD!

except that it's not just **their** wealth they're wasting—it's ours.

Which brings up another thing Clinton didn't deal with . . .

THE WARMING PLANET

Burning fossil fuels turns *oxygen* into *carbon dioxide*.

$$O_2 + CARBON \text{ (LIKE COAL OR OIL)} + (FIRE) = CO_2 + ENERGY$$

CO2 is no poison. Plants breathe it, and it keeps the planet *warm*, like the glass in a greenhouse.

Since the Industrial Revolution, we've released a lot of carbon that was once locked up in coal and oil.

By the late 1980s, the planet was clearly warming up. Warm sounds good, except for flooding, changing weather patterns, crop failures...

IT'S PERFECT RICE-GROWING WEATHER.

TOO BAD WE PLANTED WHEAT.

Clinton's vice president, Al Gore, had woken up to the dangers of global warming sooner than most. But neither he nor Clinton did much about it while they were in office. In some ways things went *backward*.

For instance, *SUVs* appeared in the 1990s. They guzzled gas in a way that hadn't been legal for passenger cars since the 1970s, thanks to a *legal loophole* that classified them as light *trucks*.

I NEED IT FOR ALL THE OFF-ROAD DRIVING I MIGHT DO ONE DAY!

IS THAT A SCRATCH?

The logical solution was to *close* the loophole, but SUVs were very profitable for the car companies.

AND THE *OIL* COMPANIES!

BUSINESS RULES (Again)

It was easy to **wish** politicians would stand up to big business, but big business had money, and political campaigns cost more every year.

"THE IDEA THAT A CONGRESSMAN WOULD BE TAINTED BY ACCEPTING MONEY FROM PRIVATE INDUSTRY OR PRIVATE SOURCES IS ESSENTIALLY A SOCIALIST ARGUMENT."

Newt Gingrich, Republican Speaker of the House (1995-1999)

An example: Way back in 1938, one Ralph Dills ran for the California legislature. His campaign cost $200.

VOTE DILLS

In 1994, Dills won his last reelection; his campaign cost **$1.2 million** (600 times more **after** inflation).

VOTE DILLS

Only very rich people and big businesses had that kind of money to give away.

MONEY DOESN'T JUST TALK; IT VOTES!

Every time two big businesses **merge**, two powerful entities become one **very** powerful one. Clinton stopped some mergers, but let others go through.

He even let Exxon and Mobil, the two biggest parts of **Standard Oil**, recombine.

JOHN D.

T.R.

Still, things could have been worse in the Clinton years....

A BRIEF RESPITE: The Clinton Prosperity

Clinton cut government waste, found some money for social programs, and expanded the **earned income tax credit** until it was an OK subsidy for the working poor.

The deficits kept shrinking, and the economy kept growing. In the late 1990s, the country caught a glimpse of **prosperity**—low unemployment, rising wages, falling crime....

EVER NOTICE HOW WHEN CRIME **FALLS** IT'S THE ECONOMY, BUT WHEN CRIME **RISES** EVERYONE BLAMES **US**?

THE LATE 1990S EVEN SAW THE FIRST **GOVERNMENT SURPLUS** SINCE THE 1960S!

Prosperity didn't mean what it once had, though. In many middle-class families both partners worked not by choice but by **necessity**. By 2000, the typical married couple with children worked **20 more weeks per year** than in 1969.

IT'S GREAT WE DON'T HAVE TO STAY HOME WITH THE KIDS ANYMORE!

ALTHOUGH I WISH I **COULD**.

I WISH MY **HUSBAND** COULD.

Another way to cope: **Work longer** before getting an apartment, before getting married, before buying a house....By the time people were on their feet and ready to start a family, it could be **too late**.

FERTILITY CENTER

WE DIDN'T REACH **ECONOMIC** MATURITY UNTIL **PHYSICAL** MATURITY HAD PASSED.

If the middle class was struggling, what of the poor? Author Barbara Ehrenreich, unlike most people who write about the poor, tried **living their life**.

FASTER!

She found it nearly *impossible* to get ahead, even with two jobs, even in a boom.

FASTER!

When people have to work more than one low-wage job, some hard-won protections become meaningless.

35 HOURS/ WEEK, NO OVERTIME

35 HOURS/ WEEK, NO OVERTIME

SLOP BURGERS

These low-wage jobs were all many people could get. In 2000, the country's biggest *employer* was no longer GM, with its middle-class union jobs—it was Manpower Inc., a *temp agency*.

And the biggest *corporation* was Walmart, whose workers were so poorly paid that they sometimes qualified for *welfare*.

WALMART EVEN HELPS US *APPLY* FOR WELFARE.

SO TAXPAYERS PAY SOME OF OUR WAGES!

"IT'S NOT A FUN SITUATION. IT'S DEMEANING."
—WALMART WORKER QUOTED IN THE DOCUMENTARY
WAL-MART: THE HIGH COST OF LOW PRICE

STILL, THE CLINTON ECONOMY WAS THE HEALTHIEST ECONOMY MOST PEOPLE COULD REMEMBER.

Conservatives weren't about to give Clinton the credit, so they puffed up Alan Greenspan.

Really, after 1994 Greenspan mostly just kept exchange rates **stable**.

He does deserve credit for that. Greenspan was under constant pressure to **raise** rates.

UNEMPLOYMENT IS BELOW 6%! THAT'S *TOO LOW*!

WORKERS WILL DEMAND HIGHER WAGES!

THAT'LL SPARK INFLATION!

Greenspan had figured out that with Clinton shrinking the deficit, he could relax.

I'M EASING UP ON THE GAS; YOU CAN EASE UP ON THE BRAKE.

HMM.

He also saw that **productivity**, a worker's output per hour, was rising. And if workers produce more, it's OK if they get higher wages.

A LITTLE HIGHER, ANYWAY.

It's true that in the long run, workers can **earn** more only if they **make** more. But wages had stagnated, even as productivity kept rising. That meant businesses paid less wages per unit produced. The savings hadn't shown up in lower prices, which leaves only **profit**. Again, Adam Smith had it right:

WAGES vs. PRODUCTIVITY
(1951 = 100)

260
220
180
140
120
100

1951   1973   1995

PRODUCTIVITY
WAGES

"OUR MERCHANTS AND MASTER-MANUFACTURERS COMPLAIN MUCH OF THE BAD EFFECTS OF HIGH WAGES IN RAISING [PRICES]. THEY SAY NOTHING CONCERNING THE BAD EFFECTS OF HIGH PROFITS. THEY ARE SILENT WITH REGARD TO THE PERNICIOUS EFFECTS OF THEIR OWN GAINS. THEY COMPLAIN ONLY OF THOSE OF OTHER PEOPLE." —ADAM SMITH

In other words:

WE *MAKE* MORE PIE, BUT WE DON'T *GET* MORE PIE.

WHERE'S THE REST OF THE DAMN PIE?

CHLORP! GLOMMP

Productivity did rise **faster** in the 1990s than it had in a while, maybe because people were working hours they weren't being paid for. Or maybe because of **computers**, and especially the **Internet**.

THE "NEW ECONOMY"

It had been clear for a long time that someday there would be a big network of computers. This network could easily have been **centralized**, run by government or big business.

But during the Cold War, the U.S. military set up a **decentralized** computer network.

HARDER TO NUKE!

Over the years, government, businesses, and universities joined this network. In the early 1990s, the World Wide Web of linked documents was developed, and suddenly the network—now called the Internet—was wide-open.

INFORMATION IS FREE!

The decentralization and low cost made the Internet a **level playing field** . . .

I CAN USE IT!

SO CAN I!

where big corporations could show how agile and entrepreneurial they were.

AND I WILL! AS SOON AS I SET UP A SUBCOMMITTEE TO REPORT TO A TASK FORCE TO INVESTIGATE THE POSSIBILITY OF FORMING A WORKING GROUP TO . . .

While established businesses dithered, new companies staked out claims in this new territory.

Some of these new "dot-coms" did very well, and investors woke up to their potential. In 1995, a company called Netscape, which made an early Web browser, first sold its stock to the public in an *initial public offering*. Netscape expected to get $28 a share; by day's end, its stock was at $75 a share.

WALL ST.

Things got silly quickly, but at least money was flowing from savings to real investment instead of the other way. And Wall Street was right: The Internet *was* revolutionary.

That's because most technologies extended our *physical* powers.

Very few extended the power of our *brains*.

The jump from separate computers to the Internet may prove to be as important as the jump from writing to printing.

But revolutions take *time*; Internet stocks traded as if the future had *arrived*.

TEN!

A HUNDRED!

FIVE HUNDRED!

All the focus on the Internet's potential to revolutionize *commerce* could obscure its potential to revolutionize *other* areas.

THE NEW PUBLIC

On pages 152-154, we saw economies of scale lead to a small elite providing information, news, and entertainment to everyone else.

Cable TV, with its many channels, might have changed that, if each channel had a different owner. But by the late 1990s, a few corporations owned almost *all* media.

The Internet was different.

For the first time in decades, regular people could hear each other, answer back, argue...

BEATS YELLING AT THE TV!

and *organize themselves* without much in the way of hierarchy.

I'LL GO IF YOU ALL GO.

I'LL GO IF YOU ALL GO.

I'LL GO IF SOMEONE ELSE GOES.

LET'S GO.

Thanks to the Internet, decentralized organizations seemed to spring up out of nowhere; many people were surprised when a *protest movement* suddenly showed up in force, in 1999, in *Seattle*.

They were there to protest a meeting of the World Trade Organization (WTO), the successor to the General Agreement on Tariffs and Trade from page 134.

THE WTO HAD THE SAME MISSION AS THE GATT: PROMOTE LOW TARIFFS, LOTS OF TRADE— IN OTHER WORDS, *GLOBALIZATION*.

Globalization sounds pretty *good*, actually. To see what the protesters were protesting, we have to pop back to the 1980s.

ONE SIZE FITS NONE: Globalization

In the 1980s, when Paul Volcker made dollars **scarce**, many Third World countries had trouble paying back loans that they'd taken out in the easy-money 1970s. The *International Monetary Fund* came to help.

YOU CAN USE *THIS* LOAN TO PAY BACK THE *BANK'S* LOAN!

SO YOU'RE BASICALLY GIVING MONEY TO YOUR OWN BANK.

AND THE BANK LENT THAT MONEY TO THE DICTATORS WHO OPPRESSED US FOR DECADES. WHY DO *WE* HAVE TO PAY BACK?

YOU'RE WELCOME!

This help came with conditions called **structural adjustments**.

IF YOU WANT THE MONEY, YOU HAVE TO SHOW THAT YOU'LL HANDLE YOURSELVES *RESPONSIBLY* THIS TIME AND NOT GET INTO TROUBLE AGAIN.

IMF

By the 1980s, the IMF was full of **neoliberals**. Structural adjustment came down to **adopting neoliberalism**.

Sell public services to private owners (*privatization*)

Cut taxes on rich people and corporations

Cut public spending (except military spending) to keep the budget balanced

Deregulate everything

Laissez-faire!

Structural adjustment was hard to refuse: The World Bank, private lenders, businesses, the U.S. Treasury, even aid donors would all steer clear of a country that the IMF said was unsound.

Still, people **hated** structural adjustment, and the IMF knew it. So part of the program was **protected democracy**, in which the economic program was protected **from** democracy.

YOU CAN ELECT ANYONE YOU WANT TO RUN THE GOVERNMENT, BUT THE GOVERNMENT CAN'T TOUCH THE ECONOMY!

GOVERN-MENT

ECONOMY

DO YOU EVEN UNDERSTAND WHAT DEMOCRACY *IS*?

Forcing your ideas on others is wrong even if the ideas work. But structural adjustment often triggered *economic crises*, so countries needed *more help*, which came with *more conditions*, conditions that got incredibly *specific*.

Mexico:
  Raise university fees

Haiti:
  Cap the minimum wage

Tanzania:
  Sell the water utility to a private company

IMF

WORLD BANK

More crises would follow, and so on.

"The middle class rapidly disappeared and the garbage heaps of the increasingly rich few became the food table of the multiplied population of abjectly poor."
—Fidelis Balogun, Nigerian writer
  (Nigeria got IMF help in the 1980s)

By the late 1980s, neoliberals should have *noticed* how often their ideas failed (or, as in Chile, "succeeded" only after they were *abandoned*). But, no.

ANY PROBLEMS ARE MERELY TEMPORARY.

THE *TRANSITION* MAY BE PAINFUL, BUT IT'LL ALL BE WORTH IT IN THE LONG RUN.

THOSE EXACT ARGUMENTS WERE ONCE USED TO EXPLAIN AWAY THE FAILURES OF *MARXISM*. FOR THAT MATTER, BOTH MARXISTS AND NEOLIBERALS FOCUSED ON HOW AN IDEAL ECONOMY *SHOULD* WORK, NOT HOW A *REAL* ECONOMY *DOES* WORK; BOTH ALSO THOUGHT THEIR IDEAL COULD BE ACHIEVED BY *REMOVING THE STATE*.

Furthermore, both *dreamed up* their ideal by mistaking David Ricardo's model economy—or a derivative of it—for the real world. (Told you Ricardo was important.)

Heck, it could be hard to say which was which.

A CRISIS WILL TRIGGER A REVOLUTION, AFTER WHICH THE STATE WILL WITHER AWAY.

"THE POLITICAL ECONOMY OF DEEP CRISES TENDS TO YIELD RADICAL REFORMS WITH POSITIVE OUTCOMES."
"INDEED, AS THE CRISIS DEEPENS THE GOVERNMENT MAY GRADUALLY WITHER AWAY."

Michael Bruno, chief economist of development economics at the World Bank (1991-1996)

Engels

So neoliberals' unimpressive results didn't slow them down. In the 1990s, when the Soviet Union fell, the ex-Soviet world went straight from one Ricardo-based ideology to another.

FREE THE *ENTIRE ECONOMY, ALL AT ONCE!*

IT'S *SHOCK THERAPY!*

IT WORKS EVERY TIME!

REALLY?

The result was more shock than therapy, especially in Russia. A few *oligarchs* wound up owning the big industries...

while everyone else got economic collapse, failing basic services, even falling *life span*. A joke went:

EVERYTHING THE COMMUNISTS SAID ABOUT COMMUNISM WAS *FALSE*. EVERYTHING THEY SAID ABOUT CAPITALISM WAS *TRUE*.

When Russia's parliament looked ready to try something else, Russia's experiment with democracy was *ended* (with Western blessing).

Boris Yeltsin, president of Russia and ally of the oligarchs, attacking the Russian parliament in 1993

OF COURSE, THE EX-SOVIET WORLD WAS SHAKY *BEFORE* NEOLIBERALS GOT THERE. FOR THAT MATTER, THE IMF GENERALLY DIDN'T SHOW UP UNLESS A COUNTRY WAS *ALREADY* IN TROUBLE. BUT STILL, I'M AMAZED HOW THE IMF AND OTHER INSTITUTIONS KEPT GETTING THINGS *WRONG*.

without the institutions that had evolved to keep them in check, like unions, environmental protections, workplace safety laws, wage and hour protections . . .

"The typical factory . . . in a country such as Honduras or Nicaragua, China or Bangladesh, is surrounded by barbed wire. Behind its locked doors, mainly young women workers are supervised by guards who beat and humiliate them on the slightest pretext and who fire them if a forced pregnancy test comes back positive. Each worker repeats the same action—sewing on a belt loop, stitching a sleeve—maybe two thousand times a day. They work under painfully bright lights, for twelve- to fourteen-hour shifts, in over-heated factories, with too few bathroom breaks and restricted access to water (to reduce the need for more bathroom breaks), which is often foul and unfit for human consumption in any event."
—Joel Bakan, *The Corporation* (2004)

It was easy to evade responsibility by contracting out the work.

I CAN'T KEEP TRACK OF HOW MY STUFF GETS MADE!

I GUESS YOU'RE TOO BUSY KEEPING TABS ON MY PURCHASES, MY CREDIT, MY INTERNET USE, EVERY KEYSTROKE YOUR EMPLOYEES MAKE, HOW LONG THEY SPEND IN THE BATHROOM, WHAT'S IN THEIR URINE . . .

SOMETIMES THE SAVINGS WERE PASSED ALONG TO CONSUMERS. ELECTRONICS, FOR INSTANCE, OFTEN SOLD FOR THEIR COST PLUS A SMALL MARKUP.

BUT BY NOW ADVERTISING WAS SO EFFECTIVE THAT MOST OF THE VALUE OF SOME PRODUCTS CAME FROM THEIR *IMAGE*.

That's why a DVD player can cost less than a pair of sneakers that cost only a few bucks to make: With the sneakers, you're buying an *image* more than a shoe.

CHARISMA!

+ SEX! SEX! SEX!

He meant *profit*

RESPECT!→

YOU MUST HAVE IT!

"There's no value to making things anymore." – Phil Knight, CEO of Nike

Whether goods were cheap or overpriced, the workers who made them couldn't afford them; the goods were sold in *rich* countries.

Trade barriers would wreck the whole arrangement, which brings us back to the World Trade Organization. It was established by treaty in 1995 as a forum to settle trade disputes. One common type of dispute: whether national laws were really *dirty tricks* like the restrictions on *tomato size* we saw on page 187. If they were, the WTO could *void* them.

But the WTO met behind **closed doors**, where powerful First World interests had their way with it.

This sort of thing is known as *policy laundering*— putting policies that would never get through the normal legislative process into treaties, which then become the law of the land.

All of which meant that the protesters in Seattle were on to something.

WE'RE NOT AGAINST GLOBALIZATION; WE'RE AGAINST THE *WAY* IT'S HAPPENING.

They certainly seemed to have struck a nerve.

The people in the WTO meeting— the central bankers, business leaders, and politicians— didn't like the attention; they responded with **more secrecy** and **harsher security** at later meetings.

TRUST US

POLICE

THE PROTESTS DIDN'T **STOP** THE MEETINGS, BUT AT LEAST THEY BROUGHT ATTENTION TO THE FACT THAT THERE **WAS** A SMALL CROWD OF PEOPLE WHO WERE TRYING TO DECIDE THE ECONOMIC FATE OF THE WORLD WITHOUT ASKING THE REST OF US.

For a while, it looked as if this would be the economic issue of the 21st century: a globalized corporate elite against a globalized, decentralized resistance movement.

But the movement had trouble just getting its message out; most people still got their news from the regular old media.

THE SEATTLE PROTESTERS ARE SIMPLY "AGAINST WORLD TRADE"!

THOSE WEIRDOS!

That quote was from ABC News, owned by Disney, which makes merchandise in Third World sweatshops.

Politics mostly went on as usual. In fact, in the 2000 election, politics took a rather large step **backward**. The new president was George W. Bush, son of George H. W.

MORE REAGANOMICS: Bush II

President George W. Bush's big priority: *tax cuts*.

SURPLUS

WE CAN *AFFORD* A TAX CUT!

But, in 2001, the Internet bubble popped.

GO WALL STREET!

HOORAY FOR ME

During the Internet bubble, Wall Street had rewarded telecommunications companies that built capacity to match the *hype*, not the reality.

WHY ARE WE DOING THIS?

TO KEEP OUR STOCK PRICE HIGH!

THE RESULT WAS NEARLY UNBELIEVABLE.

"Wall Street raised $1.3 trillion of telecom debt and sparked a $1.7 trillion merger spree, bagging $15 billion in fees for the effort. Then, the accumulation party ended. The industry collapsed amidst a $230 billion pile of bankruptcies and fraud, wiping out $2 trillion in market value and defaulting on $110 billion of debt (half of all defaults). Telecom execs pocketed $18 billion before they cut 560,000 jobs. And in 2003, over 96% of the capacity built lies dormant."
—Nomi Prins, former investment banker

PEOPLE *FORGET* SUCH FIASCOS WHEN THEY PRAISE THE "MAGIC OF THE MARKET." BUT IF WE'D HANDED OUR TELECOMS TO THE MOST HAM-FISTED SOVIET COMMISSAR WE COULD FIND, I DOUBT HE COULD HAVE DONE WORSE.

I WOULD HAVE DONE BETTER, COMRADE!

Another problem with leaving things to the market: Wall Street will fire managers if they don't make high profits, and will reward them handsomely if they do.

But Wall Street mainly knows what management tells it. So managers have a big incentive to *lie*.

WE DID GREAT!

PROFITS

CHECK

WALL ST.

WALL ST.

HERE'S YOUR BONUS!

In the early 2000s, it turned out that many companies, including Enron (the seventh-largest company in America), had made up their profits, with the help of sleazy accountants and stock analysts.

THE ACCOUNTANTS AND ANALYSTS HAD **CONFLICTS OF INTEREST** SIMILAR TO THE ONES THE GLASS-STEAGALL ACT (PAGE 117) PREVENTED. BUT THE GOVERNMENT NO LONGER CARED; GLASS-STEAGALL ITSELF HAD BEEN **REPEALED** IN 1998.

Some reforms were enacted, like the **Sarbanes-Oxley Act** (2002), which made CEOs personally sign off on their corporations' financial statements (CEOs fought it).

I THOUGHT YOU WERE FOR PERSONAL RESPONSIBILITY?

But the most obvious reform—making corporations report the same profits to shareholders and the tax man—didn't even come up. So corporations still had big incentives to lie to both.

WE MADE NO PROFITS.

WE MADE **WONDROUS** PROFITS!

Anyway, the bad economic news didn't change Bush's tax-cut program, just the **justification** for it.

ECONOMY

WAIT A MINUTE . . .

THE ECONOMY'S FALTERING! WE NEED A TAX CUT TO STIMULATE IT!

The tax cuts stalled, even as rhetoric got heated.

"I THINK WE'VE DEMONSTRATED AS A PEOPLE THAT WE DON'T THINK SOME FORM OF SOCIALISM IS THE WAY TO RUN A SOCIETY."

THIS GUY HAD BEEN CEO OF THE ALUMINUM GIANT ALCOA, WHERE HE PRESIDED OVER *GOVERNMENT-SANCTIONED PRICE SUPPORTS* FOR ALUMINUM —WHICH IS "SOME FORM OF SOCIALISM."

Paul O'Neill, Bush's first secretary of the Treasury

Then Alan Greenspan came out in favor of cutting taxes. Greenspan usually spoke in gobbledygook, but this time he delivered a crystal-clear warning that Clinton's surpluses were *dangerous*.

"I'M DEEPLY WORRIED ABOUT TOO MUCH ACCUMULATION OF MONEY IN THE HANDS OF THE FEDERAL GOVERNMENT. TO THE EXTENT THAT WE RUN CASH SURPLUSES, THE GOVERNMENT WILL ACCUMULATE CASH, AND, TO GET SOME REASONABLE RETURN ON THAT MONEY, WILL HAVE TO INVEST IT IN THE MARKETS. INVESTMENTS OF THIS SIZE, BY THE GOVERNMENT, WILL POLITICIZE THE ECONOMY. NOTHING COULD BE WORSE."

GREENSPAN'S SPEECH DID THE TRICK: THE TAX CUTS WENT THROUGH, WHICH IS ONE REASON CLINTON'S SURPLUSES TURNED INTO THE DEFICITS WE HAVE TODAY.

Another reason:

We were wrong quite a good deal of the time.

—Alan Greenspan (2008)

CHAPTER 8

THE
WORLD
TODAY

(2001 ONWARD)

On September 11, 2001, terrorists flew planes into the Pentagon and the World Trade Center.

Americans united behind the government.

"DESPITE YEARS OF SCANDALS AND POLITICAL CORRUPTION, DESPITE THE STREAM OF STORIES OF PERSONAL GREED AND PIRATES IN GUCCI SCAMMING THE TREASURY, DESPITE THE RETREAT FROM THE PUBLIC SPHERE AND THE TURN TOWARD PRIVATE PRIVILEGE, DESPITE SQUALOR FOR THE POOR AND GATED COMMUNITIES FOR THE RICH, THE GREAT MASS OF AMERICANS HAVE NOT YET GIVEN UP ON THE IDEA OF 'WE, THE PEOPLE.' . . . IT'S AS IF THE CLOCK HAS BEEN ROLLED BACK TO THE EARLY SIXTIES, BEFORE VIETNAM AND WATERGATE TOOK SUCH A TOLL. . . ."
—BILL MOYERS, JOURNALIST (OCTOBER 2001)

After all, we were at war.

IT'S A WAR ON TERROR!

THE NEW COLD WAR

The War on Terror boosted *military spending* back to Cold War levels, which was odd, considering all the things that *weren't* done.

SHOULDN'T WE FUND POLICE, FIREFIGHTERS, AND HOSPITALS?

TRACK TERRORISTS' OFFSHORE MONEY, EVEN IF IT INCONVENIENCES OUR OWN TAX CHEATS?

WEAN OURSELVES OFF *OIL*, TO DRY UP THE *SOURCE* OF THEIR MONEY?

SET ASIDE MONEY TO DEAL WITH EMERGENCIES?

SHUT DOWN VULNERABLE CHEMICAL PLANTS NEAR CITIES?

HOW IS BUYING MORE TANKS A BIGGER PRIORITY THAN ALL THAT?

SHH! ORANGE ALERT! ORANGE ALERT!

MAKE SENSIBLE EVACUATION PLANS?

AND NUKE PLANTS?

This military spending got a justification when Iraq, which had nothing to do with September 11, was declared to be an *immediate threat*. Iraq was quickly occupied in 2003.

MISSION ACCOMPLISHED

Then the U.S. set about rebuilding Iraq. You might not expect the resulting fiasco to be relevant to our story, but it is: Iraq was deliberately turned into a showpiece of the *conservative program*.

CAP PERSONAL AND CORPORATE TAX RATES AT 15%, DON'T RESTRICT IMPORTS, LET OUR CORPORATIONS BUY YOUR ASSETS AND TAKE THE PROFITS OUT OF THE COUNTRY, GIVE CONTROL OF YOUR MONEY SUPPLY TO AN INDEPENDENT CENTRAL BANK, CREATE A PATENT-FRIENDLY FARM POLICY, AND PRIVATIZE EVERYTHING.

WHY DO YOU EVEN *CARE* WHAT OUR TAX RATES ARE OR HOW OUR CENTRAL BANK WORKS OR WHETHER WE USE MONSANTO'S PATENTED SEEDS?

YOU'RE WELCOME!

"The measures will represent the kind of wish list that foreign investors and donor agencies dream of for developing markets." —The Economist (approvingly) in 2003

Some conservative policies: **massively downsizing** Iraq's government and state-controlled businesses...

YOU'RE CREATING AN ARMY OF ANGRY UNEMPLOYED PEOPLE!

NOW THEY CAN BECOME ENTREPRENEURS!

laying off the entire Iraqi army...

WILL FIGHT FOR FOOD

"We were left speechless. Now there are over 400,000 trained, armed men with families that need to be fed. Where are they supposed to go? What are they supposed to do? I don't know. They certainly don't know." — Riverbend, Iraqi blogger

ignoring **public institutions**...

MUSEUM

demanding that Iraq hand its **oil** to Western oil companies...

WE'VE BEEN PUMPING AND SELLING OUR OWN OIL FOR THIRTY YEARS!

THAT'S THE PROBLEM!

creating a "democracy" with no **power**...

ELECT ANYONE YOU WANT! BUT WHOEVER YOU ELECT CAN'T TOUCH THE ECONOMY.

ECONOMY

GOVERNMENT

and letting Iraqi firms **compete** for reconstruction contracts. Wait, no, that **didn't** happen. The contracts were handed to well-connected American corporations.

Even the job of **overseeing** contracts in Iraq was farmed out to private firms.

BLESS OUR HEN HOUSE

NO PROBLEMS HERE!

Privatized **suppliers** stiffed soldiers...

SEND FOOD

SEND VEHICLE ARMOR

SEND BODY ARMOR

IRAQ

while Iraqis got pretty much **nothing**. For instance, Bechtel Corporation had a contract to rebuild the Iraqi electric grid. It mucked around a bit, got paid, and went home.

$

"It is strange how billions of dollars spent on electricity brought no improvement whatever, but in fact worsened the situation."
—An Iraqi engineer the week after Bechtel left

Militias moved into the vacuum.

POWER'S ON!

BLESS YOU!

and seemed genuinely **surprised** as things outside fell apart.

GET GOVERNMENT OFF PEOPLE'S BACKS, AND FREE MARKETS AND PROSPERITY APPEAR AUTOMATICALLY!

Meanwhile, the people in charge tended to stay in Baghdad's fortified **Green Zone**...

HELP

THE WORLD'S BIGGEST GATED COMMUNITY!

All of which shows that putting people who **hate** government in **charge** of government doesn't work out very well.

IN THE RED AGAIN

Speaking of which, back in the U.S. there was another round of **income tax cuts for the rich** (2003).

IN **WARTIME**?

"IT'S OUR DUE."

A cut in the **estate tax**, paid only by rich dead people, and a repeal of the tax on stock dividends...

R.I.P.

and a Medicare drug benefit (2004) that forced the government to pay drug companies ludicrous prices.

?

The tax cuts and wild spending emptied the Treasury...

DEFICIT

BILLIONS

600
500
400
300
200
100

2001 2002 2003

with nothing to show for it, not even a short-term boost.

MONTHLY GAIN OR LOSS OF JOBS (thousands)

200
100
0
-100
-200
-300

1/01 4/01 7/01 10/01 1/02 4/02 7/02 10/02 1/03 4/03 7/03 10/03

Alan Greenspan, still Fed chairman, frantically **cut interest rates** again and again.

INTEREST RATES

Even at low interest, borrowing didn't pick up enough.

BILL

WE'RE MAXED OUT!

Interest rates were nearing **zero** when bankers started thinking:

WHAT ABOUT LENDING TO PEOPLE WITH **BAD CREDIT**?

$

$

WHAT COULD GO WRONG?

Suddenly many people found they could borrow enough to become homeowners.

THE AMERICAN DREAM!

BANK

WHAT DOES THE FINE PRINT SAY?

NOTHING.

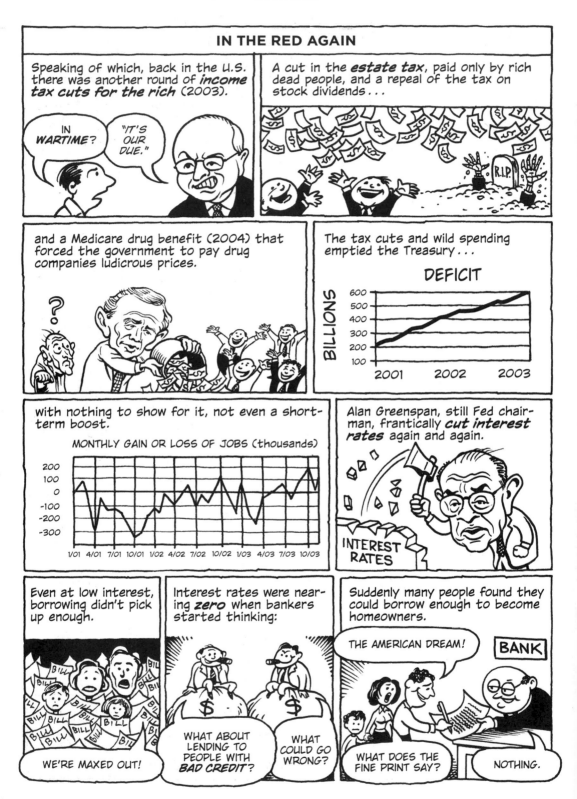

THE MORTGAGE MESS

OF COURSE, PEOPLE WITH BAD CREDIT MIGHT NOT PAY BACK THEIR LOANS. IT WOULD BE CRAZY TO *KEEP* THESE MORTGAGES.

NO PROBLEM. WE'LL SELL THEM!

BUT WHY WOULD ANYONE BUY THEM?

WELL, SEE, WE'LL BUNDLE THE MORTGAGES, SLICE UP THE BUNDLES AND DECLARE THAT ALL REPAYMENTS *GO TO* ONE SLICE FIRST, PAY OFF RATING AGENCIES TO CERTIFY THEM, BLAH BLAH BLAH . . .

The points: A bunch of bad risks became *safe-looking investments*.

The people who bought them didn't understand them . . .

WELCOME, GREATER FOOLS

WALL ST.

FOR SALE

and the *lenders* weren't the ones who had to worry about being *repaid*.

YOU'RE PREAPPROVED!

LOAN

People buying houses created *jobs* . . .

and drove up housing prices. Many home-owners felt *rich*; they borrowed more and bought more stuff.

LIVE RICHLY!

BANK

IOU

Borrowed money will take you only so far; *wages* had fallen back from their uptick in the Clinton years.

"I'm making less money this morning than at my first job 29 years ago. I got my first job in 1976 at General Motors; my starting wage was $7.55 an hour. This morning, I'm going out, 2005, I'm making seven bucks. No insurance. They call this prosperity. I call it slavery." —Gerald, laborer quoted in the TV show *30 Days*

In 1976, $7.55 would have bought what $25.83 bought in 2005.

Bankruptcies soon multiplied.

FORECLOSED   FORECLOSED   FORECLOSED   FORECLOSED

"It surprised me how hard these people struggled not to file for bankruptcy. How many...did without food, how many didn't have prescriptions filled, didn't go to the doctor; how many had had utility shutoffs. These were middle-class people, these were people with college educations, who at least once upon a time had had decent jobs, who'd bought homes, who drove relatively late-model cars, who built this sort of middle America dream. And it had fallen so far for them that they literally had lived in houses with no power on. They'd had their telephone shut off. They had no water...." —Elizabeth Warren, expert on bankruptcy law, quoted in the documentary *Maxed Out* (2006)

By 2007, some of those "safe" mortgage-based investments were **worthless**.

WHICH ONES?

WHO KNOWS?

WALL ST.

With Wall Street in trouble, the government came to the rescue. But the usual help wasn't enough.

"Too many bubbles have been going on for too long.... The Fed is not really in control of the situation." —Paul Volcker (2008)

Now: Many of these mortgages were **insured**.

MORTGAGE OWNER

INSURER

REGULAR PAYMENTS

Big payout if the borrower defaults

An insurer, basically, **bets** that nothing will go wrong; insurers are required to keep big reserves in case things **do** go wrong.

But derivatives (page 215) are bets, too; the derivative called a **credit default swap** mimics insurance, except that you don't need reserves to back them up (because derivatives are so unregulated).

MORTGAGE LENDER

REGULAR PAYMENTS

WALL ST.

Big payout if the borrower defaults

The world's biggest insurer was AIG. Its insurance division was solid, but the 20th-century financial world, where each financial company did one thing, was long gone.

AIG SR

People were happy to buy the swaps because everyone knew AIG's insurance division had big reserves.

A division of AIG was big into derivatives, especially credit default swaps.

AIG JR

This all went well at first. AIG's derivatives division sold **more** credit default swaps, far beyond what the insurance division's reserves could cover. AIG was well set up to profit—as long as nothing went wrong.

Overall, this didn't make sense for AIG, but it made sense for some people *in* AIG.

BIG PROFITS **THIS YEAR** MEANS BIG BONUSES FOR US.

BONUSES WE DON'T HAVE TO GIVE BACK NO MATTER WHAT HAPPENS NEXT YEAR.

When things did go wrong, AIG's reserves couldn't begin to cover its losses, especially because some of those reserves were **mortgages**.

POOF!

The government stepped in and bailed out AIG, which really meant handing taxpayer money to AIG's **betting partners**, which were powerful Wall Street firms.

PRIVATIZED PROFITS AND SOCIALIZED LOSSES!

Still, despite all the government help, by late 2008 lending was freezing up.

WE DON'T TRUST YOU, AND WE DON'T TRUST ONE ANOTHER!

LOAN APPLI-CATION

CAN'T ARGUE WITH THE SECOND PART OF THAT.

CRASH

IN TONIGHT'S PERFORMANCE OF "PAGE 112, PANEL 7," THE ROLE OF ANDREW MELLON WILL BE PLAYED BY TREASURY SECRETARY HENRY PAULSON AND FED CHAIR BEN BERNANKE.

As panic spread, the Treasury dumped hundreds of billions on Wall Street through the *Troubled Assets Relief Program* (TARP)—not to mention $2 trillion worth of loans from the Fed with *no* oversight.

It was true that a big enough infusion of money would solve Wall Street's immediate problems. Much the same way that *heroin* solves a *junkie's* immediate problems.

WALL ST.

After all, the financial system *depended* on a flow of money from the real economy even in *normal* times.

FOREIGN CASH COMING IN FOR CAPITAL, TO BALANCE MONEY GOING OUT FOR GOODS

STOCK BUYBACKS (ALMOST $70 BILLION IN JULY 2007 *ALONE*)

LUDICROUS DIVIDENDS (SEE BELOW)

PERIODIC BAILOUTS

TAX BREAKS AND SUBSIDIES

INTEREST ON THIRD-WORLD DEBTS

INTEREST FROM THE GOVERNMENT

INTEREST FROM THE REST OF US

MONEY DIVERTED FROM PENSION FUNDS, R & D, ETC.

RESERVED FOR OUR SOCIAL SECURITY CONTRIBUTIONS

An example regarding dividends: GM started losing money in 2005 but paid dividends well into 2008. Then *taxpayers* had to bail GM out.

THE WORLD CRISIS

The questioning wasn't confined to the U.S. Although we call the financial world "Wall Street," by the 2000s it really was the financial *world*—it spanned the globe. So the *crash* was global. Let's take a look, starting in *Iceland*.

Iceland's problems started with an unusually sudden and far-reaching deregulation of the financial sector (2001)...

leading to a spectacular bubble...

and a spectacular crash

By 2009:

WE'LL HELP! WITH TERMS, OF COURSE.

CONTRACT

X—

IMF

Iceland accepted some terms, but not all—for instance, foreign banks **weren't** paid back for their losses.

IMF

LETTING FINANCE FAIL TO SOME DEGREE HELPED ICELAND ESCAPE THE WORST CONSEQUENCES OF THE CRASH; BY 2011 THE ICELANDIC ECONOMY WAS RECOVERING.

GREECE TOOK A DIFFERENT PATH.

Greece found itself in debt trouble, and it couldn't just print the money; it **shared** its money (the euro) with other countries.

WE'LL BAIL YOU OUT, WITH FRANCE'S AND GERMANY'S HELP!

YOU MEAN BAIL THEM OUT.

BANKERS

IMF

CONTRACT

WHATEVER. POINT IS, YOU MUST ACCEPT *AUSTERITY*— PAYING BACK YOUR CREDITORS COMES *FIRST*.

Soon Greeks were **protesting** this austerity.

WHINERS REFUSING TO ACCEPT THE CONSEQUENCES OF THEIR ACTIONS!

One reason: Investors bore some of the blame. We can tell by looking at **how bonds work**.

A bond is an IOU, typically a promise to pay back a set amount at a set time.

BONDS FOR SALE

BONDS FOR SALE! PAY $60 NOW, GET $100 IN 10 YEARS!

The payout is the price the buyer paid, plus *interest*.

$40 interest

$60 initial price

$100 payout

If the interest rate changes, the payout doesn't change (the payout is set). Instead, the *price* changes.

Lower interest

Higher price

Higher interest

Lower price

$100 payout

Here are three factors that determine a bond's interest rate:

Payout date: How soon do buyers get back their money?

Inflation fears: What's the risk that the money itself will be worthless by the time it's paid back?

Default risk: What's the risk that the seller won't pay back at all?

Before the crash, Greek bonds paid slightly more interest than equivalent German bonds.

Equivalent in the sense that the bonds promised to pay the same amount on the same date...

and that they both paid out in euros, the unified European money that both Greece and Germany had adopted.

So the higher interest was due entirely to the higher risk of default (German bonds were considered very safe).

HIGH
INTEREST

LOW
PRICE

But Greek bonds should have paid *much* higher interest to cover that risk; that is, they should have been much cheaper.

THE FACT THAT GREEK BONDS' PRICES DIDN'T REFLECT THEIR RISK SHOWS THAT INVESTORS *HADN'T DONE THEIR HOMEWORK* BEFORE LENDING THEIR MONEY.

But then the lenders expected the borrowers to suffer all the pain.

THEY'RE THE "WHINERS REFUSING TO ACCEPT THE CONSEQUENCES OF THEIR ACTIONS"!

Which should sound familiar.

Speaking of familiar things, forcing debtor countries into *austerity* was exactly what the IMF did to the *Third World* on pages 240-241. It usually hadn't worked then.

Debt crisis is "resolved" with a bailout for creditors plus austerity for the debtor

A new debt crisis erupts

Austerity means less spending

Less spending contracts the debtor's economy, cutting the tax base and making it harder to pay back the remaining debt

AND IT DIDN'T WORK THIS TIME. BY MID-2011, DESPITE THE BAILOUT, GREECE WAS STILL ON THE EDGE OF DEFAULT, WHILE PROTESTERS WERE TRYING TO *SHUT DOWN THE COUNTRY* RATHER THAN LET THE GOVERNMENT AGREE TO MORE AUSTERITY.

ANOTHER COUNTRY HIT HARD: *IRELAND*, WHICH HAD BAILED OUT THE PRIVATE ANGLO-IRISH BANK. UNLIKE THE U.S., THE IRISH IMPOSED *CONDITIONS*.

WE'LL BAIL OUT YOUR BAD DEBTS, BUT THEN WE *OWN* YOU.

I *LIKED* THAT AT THE TIME; I FIGURED, IF WE'RE *GOING* TO BAIL OUT BANKS, THAT'S HOW WE SHOULD DO IT.

Turned out all the Irish government wound up owning was *more* bad debts it hadn't known about.

BILL

BILL

By 2011, the Irish were marching, too. Also the Spanish, the Portuguese...

Things were changing outside of Europe as well. In Latin America, several countries had more or less **expelled** the IMF . . .

and oil-rich Venezuela was taking a leadership role. Venezuela was run by Hugo Chavez, a **socialist** that the U.S. hadn't removed.

NOT FOR LACK OF TRYING.

In the Arab world, hard times strained people's patience with their dictators (the **Arab Spring**).

BY MID-2011 IT SEEMED LIKE PEOPLE ALL OVER THE WORLD WERE TAKING THINGS INTO THEIR OWN HANDS, FOR BETTER OR WORSE.

One big exception was the United States, which we left in late 2008. So let's head back there.

HOPE AND SOME CHANGE

Remember page 201, where we said that the conservative program aimed to turn the clock back to the 1920s? By the time President Barack Obama took office, 2009 looked much like 1929.

INEQUALITY

CORRUPTION

POWERLESS WORKERS

DEAD WEIGHT OF DEBT

FINANCIAL CRISIS THREATENING TO BECOME A GLOBAL DEPRESSION

OUT

IN

Still, the very fact that Bush was gone seemed to help.

JOB GAINS OR LOSSES PER MONTH

400,000
200,000
0
-200,000
-400,000
-600,000
-800,000
-1,000,000

JAN 08   JAN 09   JAN 10   SEP 10

OBAMA'S INAUGURATION

Obama didn't undo Bush's bailouts for Wall Street, but he supervised them more carefully; by 2010, the government had actually made a **profit** on the troubled assets it had bought during the panic.

OUT   IN

The Obama administration pushed through a Keynesian **stimulus program** (2009), in which the government spent money and cut taxes. It saved or created around 2 million jobs, but we'd lost more than 8 million.

HI

Obama even **reformed health care**.

YOU CAN'T EXCLUDE SICK PEOPLE, YOU CAN'T DENY CLAIMS QUITE SO OFTEN, AND YOU HAVE TO SPEND AT LEAST 80% OF THE MONEY YOU TAKE IN ON HEALTH CARE FOR THE PEOPLE WHO PAID FOR IT INSTEAD OF KEEPING IT FOR YOURSELVES.

DENIED

The health bill included reasonably generous **subsidies** for buying health insurance (and penalties for **not** buying it, so healthy people wouldn't stay out of the system until they got sick), but it left private insurers as the **only option**.

HERE YOU GO. NOW GIVE IT TO HIM.

STILL, MANY PEOPLE COULD SEE THE BENEFITS IN THEIR OWN LIVES: SICK FOLKS WHO'D BEEN DENIED INSURANCE WERE NOW COVERED, PEOPLE WHO'D BEEN UNABLE TO **AFFORD** INSURANCE COULD NOW GET IT...

OR THAT **WOULD** HAVE HAPPENED, EXCEPT THAT THE BEST PARTS OF THE DEAL DIDN'T GO INTO **EFFECT** RIGHT AWAY.

For instance, the subsidies didn't kick in until **2014**.

HEY, I NEED **TIME** FOR THE TRANSITION.

MORE TIME THAN IT TOOK TO WIN WWII?

THAT GAVE THE DEAL'S OPPONENTS A LOT OF TIME TO TRY TO **KILL** IT, EITHER THROUGH THE POLITICAL SYSTEM OR THROUGH THE COURTS. AND AS MILD AS THE REFORMS WERE, THERE WERE A LOT OF OPPONENTS.

One reason the health-care reform was so mild: The reformers assumed that health insurers compete in a free market.

BIGCORP HEALTH INSURANCE

HANK'S HEALTH INSURANCE

MARY'S HEALTH INSURANCE

I **WANT** TO CHARGE MORE, BUT I CAN'T!

But while Obama's health-care bill was being debated, economists were proving that concentrated insurance markets give insurers a lot of **power** to set their prices.

I **WANT** TO CHARGE MORE, AND I **DO**!

THAT BRINGS UP WHAT I SAID ON PAGE 200: DESPITE THE ADVANCES IN **REAL** ECONOMICS OVER THE PAST 30 YEARS, OUR ECONOMIC **POLICY DEBATES** ARE MOSTLY STUCK IN THE FREE-MARKET ECONOMICS OF THE 1970S.

Another relic of the 1970s: an obsessive focus on **inflation** rather than on unemployment, even though we didn't even **have** inflation to speak of.

WE **MIGHT** HAVE INFLATION SOMEDAY IF WE'RE NOT CAREFUL!

WE COULD USE SOMETHING TO EAT. . . .

DON'T YOU UNDERSTAND THE DANGER OF **OBESITY**?

So as Obama's stimulus wore off in 2010, the government mostly gave **banks** access to more money, money that the banks **sat** on.

WHY NOT GIVE **US** THE MONEY?

YOU MIGHT **SPEND** THE MONEY, CAUSING INFLATION.

I THINK YOU MEAN "PROSPERITY."

Many jobs that had been lost in the crash didn't come back.

JOBS LOST

PEAK

5%

LATE 2007

EARLY 2010

WOULD ~~WILL~~ WORK FOR FOOD IF I REMEMBERED HOW

270

By 2010 there was a lot to be *angry* about.

Much of this anger was **captured** by the conservative media machine we saw on pages 198-199.

"THERE IS A COUP GOING ON. THERE IS A STEALING OF AMERICA."

YEAH!

"IT HAS BEEN DONE THROUGH THE GUISE OF [OBAMA'S] ELECTION.... THIS GUY'S A MARXIST."

YEAH!

Quotes from Glenn Beck's radio show

One result was the Tea Party, which seems to have been a genuine grassroots movement . . .

. . . mixed with **astroturfing** (when big funders create movements to look like grassroots ones).

WE NEED JOBS

DOWN WITH THE FEDERAL RESERVE

CUT TAXES ON THE RICH

DOWN WITH THE LAST RESTRAINTS ON CORPORATIONS

Speaking of big funders, in January 2010, the Supreme Court *voided* hard-won restrictions on corporations' *political contributions*.

A CORPORATION IS A LEGAL PERSON, AND AS A PERSON IT HAS A RIGHT TO *FREE SPEECH!*

RRRRP

The resulting flood of money helped Republicans take the House of Representatives in the 2010 congressional elections.

LOW TAXES FOR THE RICH!

HECK, *NO* TAXES FOR THE RICH!

AUSTERITY FOR EVERYONE ELSE!

One justification for austerity: a professed concern about *fiscal responsibility*.

THE DEFICIT IS OUT OF CONTROL! WE HAVE TO CUT SPENDING!

I say "professed" because few of these politicians had objected when Bush turned Clinton's surplus into a deficit in the first place.

"REAGAN TAUGHT US THAT DEFICITS DON'T MATTER."
—DICK CHENEY

These politicians also weren't in any rush to address the *real* causes of the deficit.

SCHOOL

WE HAVE TO CUT WASTE!

Also, by law, the national debt was capped, sort of. Every time the debt approached the limit, Congress had *raised* the ceiling.

NATIONAL DEBT IN BILLIONS OF DOLLARS, 1974-2000

14,000
12,000
10,000
8,000
6,000
4,000
2,000
0

1974 1976 1978 1980 1982 1984 1986 1988 1990 1992 1994 1996 1998 2000 2002 2004 2006 2008

But in mid-2011:

THE NATIONAL DEBT IS *NEARING THE DEBT CEILING* AGAIN!

SO?

SO WE WON'T RAISE IT UNLESS YOU CUT SPENDING!

BUT IF YOU DON'T, THE FEDERAL GOVERNMENT WILL DEFAULT ON ITS DEBT AND BASICALLY *SHUT DOWN*.

YES!

The shutdown and default were averted when Democrats agreed to spending cuts and Republicans promised not to shut down the government for a few months.

A COMPROMISE!

YOU JUST GO RIGHT ON THINKING THAT.

Now, if you're thinking that conservative politicians have deliberately run up the deficit in order to make it *impossible* for the government to spend money on things they don't like, you're right. Heck, they even have a name for the tactic.

"STARVE THE BEAST!"

Antigovernment rhetoric had been good politics for decades, but when the government nearly shut down, many people started thinking more clearly about what the "beast" really was.

✓ PUBLIC HEALTH PROGRAMS
✓ ENVIRONMENTAL PROTECTIONS
✓ CONSUMER PROTECTIONS
✓ SOCIAL SECURITY
✓ ROADS   ✓ HOSPITALS
✓ MEDICARE ✓ MEDICAID
            ✓ SCHOOLS

WAIT A MINUTE....

Then on September 17, 2011, a small group of protesters showed up in Zuccotti Park, New York City—ready to occupy Wall Street.

OCCUPIED

The first occupiers were the same brand of leaderless lefties we saw protesting the World Trade Organization in Seattle in 1999 (page 245).

CRIME PAYS ON WALL ST.

But now more people knew something was wrong. The protest grew....

WHEN LIBRARIANS ARE MARCHING YOU KNOW WE'RE IN TROUBLE!

TAKE CARE OF THE 99% — NOT THE 1%

WE ARE THE 99%

GREED DESTROYS

OCCUPY WALL ST.

and spread.

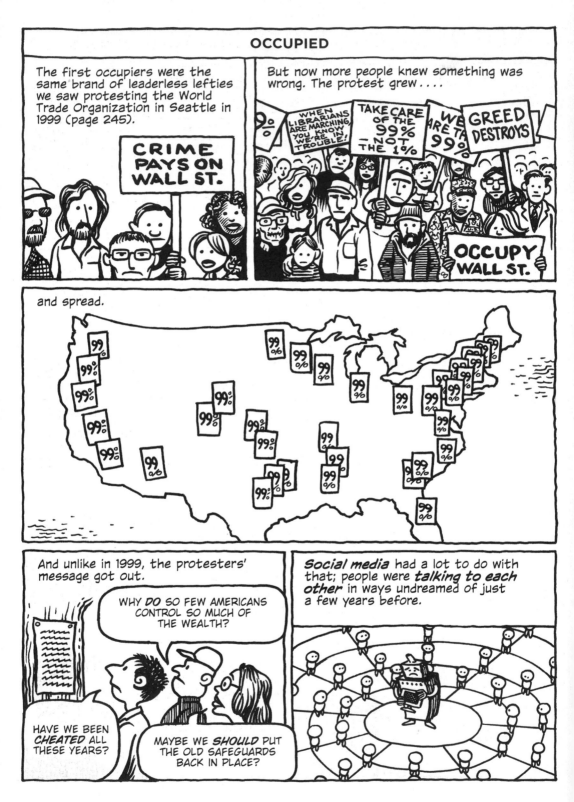

And unlike in 1999, the protesters' message got out.

WHY *DO* SO FEW AMERICANS CONTROL SO MUCH OF THE WEALTH?

HAVE WE BEEN *CHEATED* ALL THESE YEARS?

MAYBE WE *SHOULD* PUT THE OLD SAFEGUARDS BACK IN PLACE?

Social media had a lot to do with that; people were *talking to each other* in ways undreamed of just a few years before.

BLASTS FROM THE PAST

BY 2011, THE WORLD HAD A WORLD OF PROBLEMS, MANY OF WHICH SHOULD SEEM PRETTY FAMILIAR.

There were parallels to the 1970s, when an *oil crisis* had worsened a *food crisis*...

WE WANT BREAD

WE WANT BREAD

and to the robber baron era, when big businesses had escaped state controls...

while today they escape *national* controls.

For that matter, the way the World Trade Organization and other groups nullify national laws for big businesses' convenience resembles how the Supreme Court nullified *state* laws on page 87.

W.T.O.

Instead of the national oligopolies of the 19th century, we're increasingly seeing *global* ones in the 21st century. Diamonds are a good example; and **car companies** are looking more and more like a single global entity than a bunch of competitors.

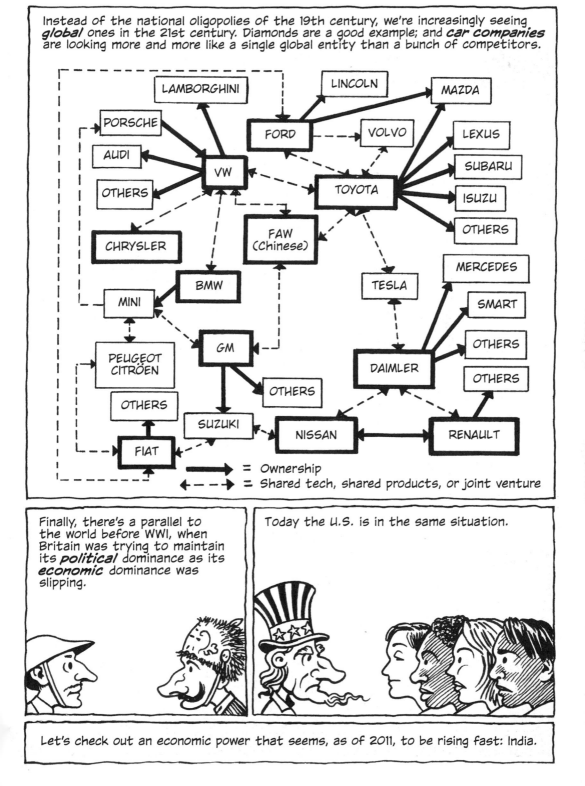

= Ownership
= Shared tech, shared products, or joint venture

Finally, there's a parallel to the world before WWI, when Britain was trying to maintain its *political* dominance as its *economic* dominance was slipping.

Today the U.S. is in the same situation.

Let's check out an economic power that seems, as of 2011, to be rising fast: India.

INDIA

India won independence from Britain in 1947. At first it had a socialist *planned economy*, but that went *too far*: Running even a small business meant endless red tape.

GROCERY

RUPEES

PLUS *BRIBES* TO AVOID *MORE* RED TAPE.

PAKISTAN

Children are still sold into slavery.

In the 1990s, India dismantled this *permit raj* system; a *boom* resulted.

Still, India is hard to summarize; even today, practically everything we've talked about, and some things we haven't, can be found in India somewhere.

MARKET-LENINISM: China

We last looked at China in 1949, when Mao Zedong's communists took over. They did OK at first.

But in the late 1950s, Mao tried to imitate Stalin's *collectivization* and *crash industrialization*. The Chinese wound up making Stalin-style sacrifices (40 million dead by one estimate) and didn't even wind up with anything to show for it.

Mao then descended into Stalin-style *paranoia*. By the 1970s, he was worshipped as a *god*, and China's rich culture was replaced by his dull writings.

Still, Mao's death in 1976 left a country that was highly literate, with remarkable *gender equality*. And in 1978, a rational leader, Deng Xiaoping, started freeing the Chinese economy and opening it to the world.

When people could work for *themselves*, they worked hard for *others*. China started a long boom that eventually brought *hundreds of millions of people* out of poverty.

COMMUNE

MY FARM—HANDS OFF!

Chinese communists freed the economy, but they had every intention of staying in charge, as the world found out in the Tiananmen Square massacre of 1989.

THE *ECONOMY'S* CHANGING, BUT THAT DOESN'T MEAN THE *POLITICAL SYSTEM* WILL CHANGE.

MARX

YES, IT *DOES*! THAT WAS MY *WHOLE POINT*!

Still, as the economy became more open, so did society.

SEE?

But this new wealth and freedom spread unevenly. China developed what can be described only as *class divisions*.

"In some factories, the [Communist] party chief is a big help; he... will intervene with great authority when workers are causing problems for you [Western investors]." —The Wall Street Journal, unintentionally defining *irony* in 1994

In the late 1990s, the West made China meet some Western standards in order to trade freely, although the choice of *which* standards was a bit odd.

YOUR SLAVE PRISONERS ARE PIRATING *COPYRIGHTED* CDS! YOU HAVE TO PAY OUR CORPORATIONS *ROYALTIES*!

OOPS! SORRY.

Chinese exports were cheap partly because China kept its *money* cheap (practically a *crime* in the neoliberal book).

Chinese goods even undersold goods from other low-wage nations, which is one reason so many Third World economies were in trouble in the 1990s and 2000s.

SORRY, WE'RE SENDING YOUR JOBS TO CHINA!

WAIT, WHAT?

SERIOUSLY?

By 2011, the Chinese economy was hard to categorize. The Chinese government seemed to be willing to try most anything.

WHATEVER WORKS!

Certainly, the Chinese never adopted the extreme free-market ideology that the West was pushing; not coincidentally, China escaped the depression of the late 2000s relatively unscathed.

BONK ★ ★ ★
BONK ★
BONK

WHY AREN'T YOU MORE LIKE ME?

Like America in the 20th century, 21st-century China was a land of new things and big things, from *flying trains* . . .

to a single electronics plant that employed around 350,000 workers (GM, at its height, employed only 700,000 workers in all its plants).

That plant made electronics for export. The workers were paid too little to buy what they made.

HMM.

HEY, THIS GUY SAYS THAT WORKERS WILL BE EXPLOITED MORE AND MORE UNTIL WE REVOLT.

MARX

This system depended on steady demand from China's customers, and the worldwide depression hurt that demand. This helps explain why, in 2011, China offered to help Europe with its financial crisis.

WE'LL BUY YOUR BONDS!

BLESS YOUR SOUL!

After all, in international trade, capital going one way will be matched by goods going the other.

STUFF

BONDS STOCKS

So really, China wasn't just offering to bail out Europe's investors; China was offering to increase its own exports.

OUR PROBLEM IS ALREADY TOO MUCH HELP FOR INVESTORS, AND NOT ENOUGH JOBS!

The Chinese were also considering *another* source of customers: the Chinese people.

YOU KNOW, IF YOU PAID YOUR WORKERS MORE, THEY COULD *BUY* WHAT YOU MAKE.

WEIRD...

But it was hard to see how *earth itself* could support that,

NEW SHOES!

which brings up another problem from the past...

OUR SICK PLANET

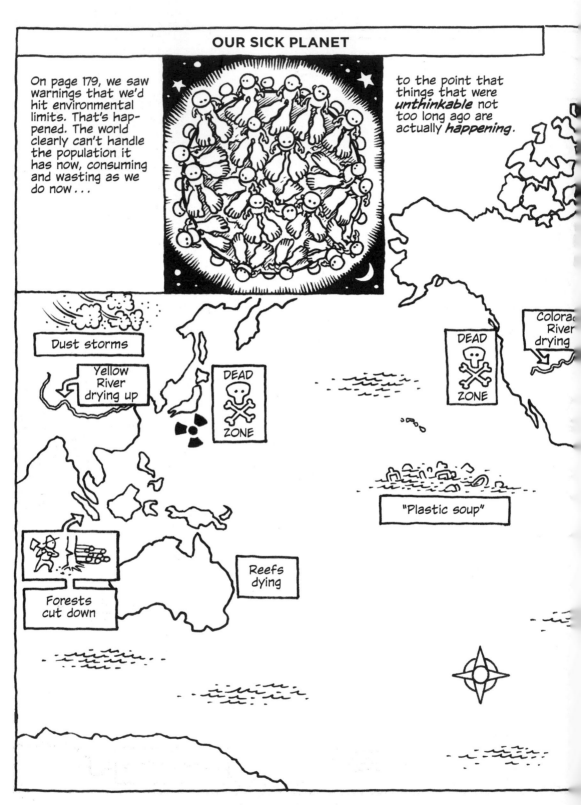

On page 179, we saw warnings that we'd hit environmental limits. That's happened. The world clearly can't handle the population it has now, consuming and wasting as we do now . . .

to the point that things that were *unthinkable* not too long ago are actually *happening*.

Dust storms

Yellow River drying up

DEAD ZONE

Colorado River drying

DEAD ZONE

"Plastic soup"

Forests cut down

Reefs dying

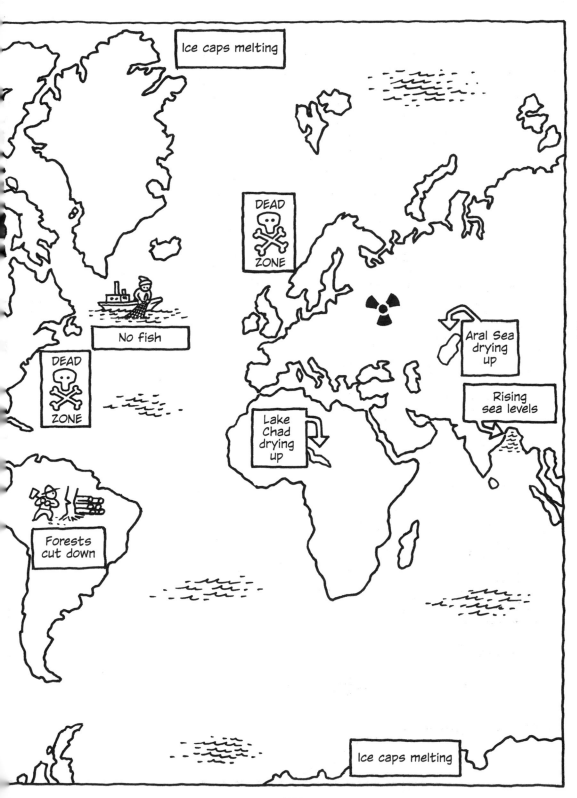

It's clearly too late to stop these problems from happening. However, it might not be too late to stop problems that are unthinkable **today**.

In fact, some people are pretty confident that **technology** will solve these problems.

AFTER WE CUT DOWN ALL THE FORESTS, PEOPLE WILL FIND SUBSTITUTES FOR WOOD.

THEN WHY NOT **PROTECT** THE FORESTS? WE'LL FIND SUBSTITUTES **AND** WE'LL STILL HAVE FORESTS.

SHUT UP!

But many of today's problems are the result of **yesterday's** ingenious solutions...

TELEVISION WILL SPREAD ENLIGHTENMENT!

PESTICIDES WILL ERADICATE BAD INSECTS ONCE AND FOR ALL!

HIGHWAYS WILL LET US ALL MOVE TO SUBURBS, ELIMINATING SLUMS!

BETTER FISHING BOATS WILL INCREASE YIELDS!

SHOPPING MALLS WILL BE DYNAMIC CENTERS OF CIVIC ENGAGEMENT!

which should make us wary of **today's** hype.

WE CAN FIX OUR PROBLEMS WITH **GENETIC MODIFICATION**!

NANOTECHNOLOGY WILL SOLVE EVERYTHING!

WITH **GEOENGINEERING**, WE'LL ADJUST THE CLIMATE AT WILL!

REANIMATED CORPSES WILL DO OUR HEAVY LIFTING!

Even if we invented a great new tech, who's to say we'd **use** it? We have plenty of technologies—ones that make environmental and economic sense—that we're barely making use of today.

We're not using them more because we haven't **decided** to. In other words, the solution is **political** as much as technological.

WHAT TO DO?

THERE'S A WHOLE RANGE OF OPINIONS ON WHAT NEEDS TO BE DONE. I CAN ONLY GIVE YOU MINE.

FIRST OFF, WE HAVE TO GET OUT OF THE CURRENT RECESSION. *KEYNESIAN SPENDING PROGRAMS* HAVE WORKED IN THE PAST. CERTAINLY, THERE'S NO END OF THINGS THAT *NEED* SOME SPENDING.

SCHOOL · FORECLOSED · FORECLOSED · FORE

THE MONEY FOR THAT SPENDING COULD COME FROM BORROWING, BUT WE'VE ALREADY BORROWED QUITE A LOT TO PAY FOR CONSERVATIVES' TAX CUTS.

It makes more sense to **undo** conservatives' tax cuts. They were supposed to create prosperity. They haven't.

Heck, we could even try new types of taxes, like a progressive tax on corporate *revenue*, not profit. Revenue is harder to hide, so even a tiny tax would bring in a lot of cash.

To avoid this tax, big corporations might *split themselves up*, limiting the power of each fragment and letting our democracy work more like it should.

TAX RATE — 3% / 2% / 1%

TAX RATE — 3% / 2% / 1%

There are a million ideas for us to debate, from a tiny tax on financial transactions (to calm Wall Street down) to simply adopting the principle that *cleaning up after yourself* should be part of the cost of doing business.

NS·O·TOY

I've put some ideas in this book, there are others at www.economixcomix.com, and you've no doubt thought of more yourself.

THE MAIN THING TO REMEMBER: WE *CAN* CHANGE THINGS. WE DIDN'T GET WHERE WE ARE BY THE IMPERSONAL WORKING OF RIGID LAWS; WE GOT HERE BY MAKING *DECISIONS*. WE CAN MAKE *NEW* DECISIONS.

Instead of arguing ourselves blue about what *should* work, we can *try* things and see what *does* work. In fact, that's what many of us are *doing*.

From keeping the pressure on Wall Street...

to *producing* energy instead of *consuming* it...

to fighting foreclosures...

THE COUNTRY BELONGS TO ALL OF US, NOT 1% OF US.

to simply choosing better banks...

MEGAMONSTER BANK

People are finding ways to work for a better, fairer economy.

OF COURSE, CHANGING THE ECONOMY IS EASIER SAID THAN DONE: IF I'VE DONE MY JOB, YOU'VE SEEN THAT MANY OF OUR PROBLEMS ARE *INTERRELATED*.

WALL ST.

GREENHOUSE EFFECT

"IT MAKES YOU HAPPY"

BUT THAT VERY INTERCONNECTEDNESS GIVES ME *HOPE*: FIXING ONE PROBLEM COULD ALSO HELP WITH OTHERS. ONCE WE GET STARTED, WE MAY WELL FIND OURSELVES SOLVING *MANY PROBLEMS AT ONCE*.

That may seem impossible, but it's been done before.

In fact, there was an opportunity to do just that in the 2008 crash, when Wall Street, big corporations, and rich folks in general were desperate for help.

WE'LL DO ANYTHING! EXCEPT SHOW GRATITUDE LATER!

WALL ST.

Some people say we missed a once-in-a-lifetime chance to fix our economy then, but these chances come along all the time; the financial world has already been bailed out more than once *since* the 2008 bailouts.

BAILOUT FOR INVESTORS IN GREEK BONDS

2008 BAILOUTS

BAILOUT FOR CREDITORS OF IRISH BANKS

WE WEREN'T READY IN 2008, BUT NEXT TIME WE COULD *REFUSE* TO HELP OUT UNLESS *WE* MAKE THE RULES.

WALL ST.

AND THERE WILL BE A NEXT TIME. ONE CAN VERY NEARLY FIX THE DATE.

THE END

GLOSSARY

BOURGEOISIE. Marx and Engels used this to mean capitalists, although it also means the middle class in general.

BUBBLE. A situation in which speculative buying raises a price, thus bringing in more and more speculators until the only thing keeping the price rising is the fact that the price is rising.

CAPITAL. The means of production. One definition is "goods that (a) we make; (b) we use to make other goods; and (c) are not used up when the goods are made." Another definition is "the money we invest to make goods."

CAPITALIST. Someone who invests capital for profit, especially someone whose main income comes from profit.

CLASSICAL POLITICAL ECONOMY. The mainstream of economic thought in the 19th century, based on the work of David Ricardo and, to a lesser degree, Thomas Malthus. Characterized by the use of abstract, simplified models rather than real-world data.

COMMERCIAL BANK. The most familiar type of banking institution, in which a bank takes deposits from customers and lends the money to other customers.

COMMUNISM. Once a synonym for socialism, now used in reference to the revolutionary branches of socialism, especially Marxism, Leninism, and Maoism.

COMPARATIVE ADVANTAGE. A model showing that both sides can always benefit from international trade. One of the premises of this model is that capitalists won't move their operations across borders; this was a reasonable assumption in the early 19th century when the model was invented, but not so much today.

CORPORATION. A legally created entity that has some of the abilities of a person, for instance, the ability to sign contracts or own property. Churches, towns, small businesses, and unions can be corporations, but this book uses the term in the popular and most important sense: a big, for-profit business that is owned by stockholders and run by managers.

DEMAND CURVE or DEMAND SCHEDULE. The part of a supply-demand chart showing how much of a product consumers will want to buy at any given price. Note that if the price changes, the quantity demanded may change, but demand doesn't change as long as the new price intersects another point on the same curve. Changes in demand are visualized by moving the curve or changing its shape.

ECONOMICS. The study of the production, consumption, and transfer of wealth.

ECONOMY OF SCALE. A savings in per-unit cost when more units are produced.

EQUILIBRIUM PRICE. The price at which the amount of a product that buyers want to buy equals the amount sellers want to sell.

EXTERNALITY. A side effect, good or bad, of a transaction. Externalities are a problem because the people deciding whether to undertake the transaction don't get all the benefits, or pay all the costs. Thus, the decisions they make for their own good may not be the best decisions overall.

FASCISM. The idea, first promulgated by Benito Mussolini, that, in an age of mass production and mass organization, democracy and individual liberty will be—and should be—replaced with an authoritarian state. Sometimes used to mean "authoritarian."

FRACTIONAL RESERVE BANKING. A fancy name for the practice of banks taking deposits, keeping some in the vaults (the fraction in reserve), and loaning out the rest.

FREE MARKET. A system in which everyone competes to provide the best products most efficiently. Although free markets must be free from excessive government regulation, removing regulation does not automatically result in a free market.

GROSS DOMESTIC PRODUCT. The value of all the legal, new goods and services sold in an economy in a year.

INFLATION. A decrease in the value of money. At any moment, some prices are going up and some are going down; inflation occurs when the overall movement is up.

INVESTMENT. Money committed to make goods, typically to sell them for a profit.

INVISIBLE HAND. A phrase used by Adam Smith to convey how a free market guides the actions of the people in it. Smith used the phrase only once, which has led several writers to say that Smith didn't intend the concept to become so prominent. But the idea of the invisible hand, if not the phrase, informs all of Smith's *Wealth of Nations*.

KEYNESIAN ECONOMICS. A macroeconomic approach that considers modifying overall demand, for instance by changing taxation and spending, to be necessary to counteract the business cycle and avoid crashes. To Keynesians, crashes are a "natural" part of the economy rather than anomalies that should be ignored until they go away.

LABOR THEORY OF VALUE. The idea that, in the long run, everything sells for a price that is essentially a measure of the labor required to make it. Originally this theory was the basis of David Ricardo's models; the idea is now advocated by Marxists.

LAISSEZ-FAIRE. The belief that leaving economic activity alone produces better results than futzing with it. Originally a reaction to mercantilism.

LAND REFORM. The process of dividing ownership of land among the people who actually work the land, instead of leaving it in the hands of a few big landlords.

LENINISM. The branch of Marxism as preached and/or practiced by Vladimir Lenin. The main distinguishing feature is a disciplined party that serves as the vanguard of the revolution.

LUDDITES. British workers who destroyed machinery in the early 19th century. By extension, anyone who dislikes technology.

MACROECONOMICS. The study of an overall economy: employment, interest rates, productivity, etc. Contrast with microeconomics.

MAOISM. Communism as preached by Mao Zedong: Key points include land reform, small-scale industry, and constant revolution.

MARXISM. Revolutionary communism; the idea that the changing capitalist economy will inevitably require political revolution, leading to a new, noncapitalist economy and a new society.

MERCANTILISM. An economic doctrine, dating to the 17th century, that treats foreign trade as an instrument to further the goals of the state. The major goal is to get foreigners' money and keep it.

MICROECONOMICS. The study of individual markets, individual firms, how consumers get the most value for their money, etc. Contrast with macroeconomics.

MIXED ECONOMY. An economy that is partly socialist and partly an unsupervised market. Most economies are mixed economies, but the specific mix varies widely.

MODEL. In economics, a model is a simplified, logical, often mathematical analysis of the economy or a part of it. Models have the advantage of being exact and rigorous. In fact, models are unquestionably true as long as their premises are met, which may be the only thing that all economists agree on. However, it's easy to forget that models' premises are often not met in the real world.

MONETARISM. A macroeconomic approach that recommends countering the business cycle by steadily increasing the amount of money in the economy. Although monetarists agree with Keynesians that the business cycle needs to be tamed, Keynesians prefer to more actively fine-tune things. Not to be confused with monetary policy, which means modifying overall demand by monetary measures (such as adjusting interest rates) instead of changing taxes and spending.

MONOPOLY. A situation in which there's only one seller of a product or service; the term can also refer to such a seller. Similar to monopsony, when there's only one buyer.

NEOCLASSICAL ECONOMICS. The branch of economics that focuses on the determination of prices by supply and demand. It became the mainstream of economics starting in the late 19th century; other ideas have nudged their way in since then, but Neoclassical economics is still going strong.

NEOLIBERALISM. A branch of economics that focuses on the connection between political and economic liberty, relying on the free market to assign resources and produce goods.

OLIGOPOLY. A group of sellers that are few enough, and cooperative enough, to limit (although usually not eliminate), the competition among them.

PHYSIOCRATS. French economists of the 18th century who believed that agriculture was the source of all wealth.

POLITICAL ECONOMY. The 19th-century term for economics; the distinction was that political economy included more of an emphasis on government and policy than the economics that followed.

PROGRESSIVE TAXATION. Taxes that take a bigger slice the more a person makes.

PUBLIC GOODS. Things like clean streets that many people want but no private entrepreneur has a reason to provide. The old distinction between public and private goods has been replaced, to some degree, by a twofold distinction depending on whether goods are excludable (whether I can stop you from enjoying them) and/or rivalrous (whether my enjoying them uses them up).

SOCIAL DARWINISM. The idea that higher socioeconomic status is a sign of better genes, and that helping people with low socioeconomic status to survive ruins the gene pool.

SOCIALISM. Most broadly, any economic activity that is undertaken cooperatively instead of competitively. This cooperation can be achieved by the collective action of the people involved or by government. Also the idea that cooperation of this kind is better than laissez-faire.

SPECULATION. The purchase of something, not because a buyer wants it for itself, but because the buyer expects to sell it for a profit when the price rises.

SUPPLY CURVE or SUPPLY SCHEDULE. The part of a supply-demand chart showing how much of a product sellers will bring to market at any given price. See demand curve.

TARIFF. A tax on imports. Tariffs can be designed to raise revenue, to keep foreign competition out, or both.

TRUST. A monopolistic or oligopolistic supercorporation of the late 19th and early 20th centuries.

UNION. An alliance of workers bargaining as a unit instead of each making separate contracts with an employer.

FURTHER READING

All of these books informed my understanding of the economy.

Joel Bakan, *The Corporation*. 2004. How the modern corporation works, and for whom. Made into a good movie.

Bryan Burrough, *The Big Rich*. 2009. The great oil men of Texas and their influence—which is pretty considerable.

E. Ray Canterbery, *A Brief History of Economics*. 2001. A clear, lively history, not just of economics, but of the economy.

James Carroll, *House of War*. 2006. A stunning history of the Pentagon, the postwar military, and the economic institutions that feed it.

Rachel Carson, *Silent Spring*. 1962. The book that touched off the environmental movement. Still a great read, and it's never been more relevant.

Ron Chernow, *The House of Morgan*. 1990. All you ever wanted to know about J. P., his crowd, and his legacy. Chernow explains obscure subjects in extreme detail while never boring his reader.

——, *Titan*. 1998. Chernow brings his talents to bear on John D. Rockefeller and Standard Oil.

Jared Diamond, *Collapse*. 2005. The environmental and economic reasons behind why societies fall apart, and how ours may soon.

Barbara Ehrenreich, *Nickel and Dimed*. 2001. What it's like to work low-wage jobs, all day every day.

Milton Friedman, *Capitalism and Freedom*. 1962. A defense of economic freedom as a precondition for political freedom.

John Kenneth Galbraith, *The Affluent Society*. 1958. How the modern economy keeps producing more stuff we don't particularly want, while shorting what we do want, in Galbraith's inimitable style.

——, *The New Industrial State*. 1967. As close as anyone's ever come to nailing down the modern industrial economy the same way Adam Smith nailed down the economy of his day.

Larry Gonick, *The Cartoon History of the Universe* and *The Cartoon History of the Modern World*. 1976–2009. One of my big inspirations. The whole story of everything from the Big Bang to the present, with a decent amount of economic history in there with everything else, in comics form.

William Greider, *One World, Ready or Not*. 1998. An excellent look at the global economy. Written in the 1990s but just as relevant today.

——, *The Soul of Capitalism*. 2004. An excellent overview of the modern economy, its problems, and how to fix them.

Friedrich Hayek, *The Road to Serfdom*. 1944. Hayek's wide-ranging writings are a pleasure to read. As happened with Adam Smith, however, free-market apologists have oversimplified his ideas to the point of parody.

Robert Heilbroner, *The Worldly Philosophers*. 1953. The lives and ideas of the great economic thinkers in sparkling prose, with all sorts of cool asides that there was no space for in *Economix*, like Veblen's womanizing, Keynes's bisexuality, Marx's carbuncles. . . .

Doug Henwood, *After the New Economy*. 2003. The tech bubble and its aftermath.

——, *Wall Street*. 1997. How the financial world really works, and for whom.

Will Hutton, *The World We're In*. 2002. A great source of info about the economy of modern Europe.

Jane Jacobs, *The Death and Life of Great American Cities*. 1961. How the combination of neglect and poor planning undid our cities after World War II.

David Cay Johnston, *Free Lunch*. 2007. The various ways that taxpayers support big businesses without getting any say in their actions.

——, *Perfectly Legal*. 2003. A meticulous account of how the tax code has been corrupted to hand all the money to the rich.

Naomi Klein, *No Logo*. 2000. How corporate marketing has penetrated into our culture and taken over the economy. Today, marketers use it as a handbook.

——, *The Shock Doctrine*. 2007. How the same free-market ideology was forced on country after country, and the insane consequences.

Paul Krugman, *The Conscience of a Liberal*. 2007. Krugman finally embraces the "economic heresy" that power matters. Essential.

——, *The Great Unraveling*. 2003. A collection of Krugman's essays showing how the early George W. Bush administration did its best to dismantle the New Deal.

Amory Lovins, Hunter Lovins, and Paul Hawken, *Natural Capitalism*. 1999. How taking care of the environment pays better than all this waste, which is, after all, waste.

Karl Marx and Friedrich Engels, *The Communist Manifesto*. 1848. A short, clear intro to Marx's and Engels's ideas.

Donella Meadows, Jørgen Randers, and Dennis Meadows, *Limits to Growth: The 30-Year Update*. 2003. A sober 1972 look at how the world economy would be hitting environmental limits, updated to show just how very accurate it was.

Ralph Nader, *Unsafe at Any Speed: The Designed-In Dangers of the American Automobile*. 1965. How car companies, which used to redesign their cars to look snazzier every year, didn't bother to improve the engineering or safety because nobody forced them to. If you've ever walked away from a car crash, this book may have been the reason.

John Perkins, *Confessions of an Economic Hit Man*. 2004. How corporations twist Third World governments' arms until they buy big, useless projects (with money lent by other corporations), written by one of the people who did the twisting.

Kevin Phillips, *Wealth and Democracy: A Political History of the American Rich*. 2003. The history of the American ruling class since its birth after the Civil War.

Jacob Riis, *How the Other Half Lives*. 1890. The classic look at the slums of the 19th century, still sadly relevant.

Eric Schlosser, *Fast Food Nation*. 2001. Sinclair's *The Jungle* for modern times. If you want to break that Big Mac habit, this is the book for you.

——, *Reefer Madness*. 2003. The shadow economy: drugs, porn, and illegal work.

Adam Smith, *The Wealth of Nations*. 1776. The granddaddy of them all. Smith's style can wear on modern readers, and he was never much for organizing his ideas, but nobody else has ever matched his mastery of both the finest details and the big picture. Always keep in mind that it's a very accurate description of the economy as it was when the book was published, not the world of today.

Joseph Stiglitz, *Globalization and Its Discontents*. 2002. A former chief economist of the World Bank, and Nobel laureate, skewers the globalization agenda of the 1990s.

Alexis de Tocqueville, *Democracy in America*. 1835 and 1840. Tocqueville means "equality in America." A thoughtful, perceptive description of the America that was lost with the rise of the trusts.

Thorstein Veblen, *The Theory of the Leisure Class*. 1899. There was no room for Veblen in *Economix*, but this is his masterpiece—a brilliant, wicked look at how primitive the most "evolved" of us are, in hysterically overdone prose. Who else could call yappy lapdogs "canine monstrosities" and get away with it?

Howard Zinn, *A People's History of the United States*. 1980. American history through the eyes of the common people. There's a graphic adaptation, too!

ACKNOWLEDGMENTS

Writing this book involved years of solitary reading, thinking, and writing; the following people made those years bearable.

I never would have started on this book without Pam Berenbaum and JaneAnne Murray.

Ashley, Sheeba, Sanjay, Sarah, and Sindhu at Greenwoods opened their home to me as I started writing. Priya, Sanjay, and Sanjay at the Teapot; Sunny, Alpa, Silvan, Hiren, Tsirin, Lucas, Diego, Bansari, and Bindu at the Coffee Pot; and Holly, Antone, Allison, and Michele at Bisco let me use their establishments as offices.

My family provided suggestions, connections, and plain old encouragement when I worried that the whole project was insane. Encouragement also came from Stephen Dubner, Kendlyn Dias, Matthew Franklin, Ilene Richman, Nina Paley, Gary Marcus, Dean Haspiel, Eleanor and Michelle Horowitz, Mia Lipsit, Vanessa Weiman, Taylor Janis, John Bossen, Betty Zsoldos, John Glenn, Don Kalb, and Ken Hale.

My agents, Judith Hansen and Sui Mon Wu, took on a half-finished book from an unknown author and stayed enthusiastic as I finished; they also introduced me to Dan Burr's work.

I can't thank Dan Burr enough for his amazing illustrations; they look even better than what I had in my head. Thanks also go to Henrik Rehr, who first turned my words into pictures, as well as Chris Butzer, S. Y. Choi, Big Time Attic, and J. P. Coovert for their excellent samples.

Charlie Kochman at Abrams believed in the book enough to buy it, back when I was still unsure of what I'd created. Sheila Keenan, my editor, took my gloppy first draft and guided it to completion.

James K. Galbraith, Morten Rønningen, Hege Karlsen, David Ellis Dickerson, Michele Passalacqua, Milan Gagnon, and Judith Weinblatt saw early versions and didn't use the term "Unabomber Manifesto" in their comments.

Larry Gonick, whose incredible nonfiction comics inspired my own, provided valuable comments.

Ian Akin and Brian Garvey, artists and letterers, pulled my butt out of the fire as schedules became tight.

Tracy Rowland patiently endured my anxiety attacks when things went wrong and my manic joy when things went right. She is very awesome.

Finally, my eternal gratitude goes to Timothy Guinnane, who patiently read the manuscript and saved me from too many errors to count, and then did the same thing with the first sketched version. Olivier Giovannoni caught several errors that had crept in at a later stage. Any remaining errors are my own fault.

—M. G.

I want to acknowledge the important contributions Debra Freiberg, my wife and art partner, made to the production of this project. The lettering, as well as art touch-ups and referencing, all bear her stamp of quality control.

I would also like to give hearty and sincere thanks to Judy Hansen, and to the late Dave Schreiner for his initial encouragement long ago, and, of course, to Michael Goodwin.

—D. E. B.

ABOUT THE AUTHOR

MICHAEL GOODWIN is a freelance writer who has always loved comics and history, partly thanks to an early exposure to Larry Gonick's *Cartoon History of the Universe*. His interest in history developed into a curiosity about the economic forces that underlie much of history, and he eventually sat down with some economics texts. In his initial reading, Michael thought he caught glimpses of a story, a story nobody seemed to be telling.

That idea was little more than a hunch at first, but as he immersed himself in the subject, Michael realized that there was in fact a story there, and that someone needed to tell that story in an accessible manner. He brought a stack of books to a small town in India, settled in, and started reading, researching, and writing. The result is this book.

Michael has spent several years in China as well as India; his previous efforts include interpreting Chinese, writing comedy, shooting photographs, working at disaster relief, dealing art (ineptly), and writing about medicine. Like many freelance writers, he lives in New York City with two cats.

ABOUT THE ARTIST

DAN E. BURR was born to this work, as examples of early attempts at comic strip–like continuity exist from his infancy. (Drawing pictures was "in the family," so the influence to do so was ever present.)

After time spent mainly working in commercial art, Dan began to wade into the comic book field. The breakthrough project was his collaboration with author James Vance on the graphic novel *Kings in Disguise* and its sequel, *On the Ropes*. *Kings* won several Eisner and Harvey Awards and garnered praise from *Time*, *Entertainment Weekly*, and the *New York Times Book Review*, among others.

Dan has illustrated historical pieces for DC Comics, Kitchen Sink Press, and Eureka Productions' Graphic Classics series. His work in *Economix* was influenced by the artists who worked on Harvey Kurtzman's *MAD*; by caricaturists like David Levine and Al Hirschfeld; and by the work of the late fifties/early sixties Hanna-Barbera staff.

Dan lives in Milwaukee with his wife and art partner, Debra Freiberg.

INDEX